"Leroy Barber dreams big dreams for our generation—dreams that have the power and potential to change the world forever. This book will inspire anyone who wants to move beyond the ordinary toward an extraordinary life lived for God."

MARGARET FEINBERG, author of *Scouting the Divine* and *The Organic God*

"*Everyday Missions* is anything but an everyday book. Leroy Barber speaks directly and convincingly into the lives of ordinary people, challenging us to consider commitments that have extraordinary impact. Provoking—in the very best sense of the word—this hopeful, can-do book inspires readers to risk pursuing their created purpose and discover their true source of meaning."

BOB LUPTON, president, FCS Urban Ministries, Atlanta, Georgia

"Leroy Barber has earned the right to be heard by helping hundreds of young college graduates discern how to live out the Christian life in lay vocations. This book taps into the wisdom he has accumulated over the years, along with his biblical insights as to how those of us in the pew can become radical followers of Jesus in our everyday lives."

TONY CAMPOLO, professor emeritus, Eastern University

"In an age when missional engagement has been reduced to dramatic short-term immersion experiences, Leroy Barber challenges us to live a consistent life of credible compassion. In *Everyday Missions* Leroy reframes the conversation about mission by illuminating the need to live missionally. He reflects on a life of service, not one that merely talks a prophetic game but one that embodies love. *Everyday Missions* is provocative and challenging, inspiring and accessible—a clarion call in an age of vocational confusion, this book will nurture your imagination to doing good better."

CHRIS HEUERTZ, international director of Word Made Flesh, and author of *Friendship at the Margins*

"Some of the best things in church history, and some of the worst, have been done in the name of 'missions.' It's one of those words we need to dust off, reclaim and re-envision so that we are spreading the real gospel—not the white man's gospel, not the prosperity gospel, not the American gospel, not the fluffy, do-it-yourself gospel, not the empire's gospel or the colonialist's gospel—but the gospel of Jesus, the gospel that is always good news to the poor, the gospel that comes with a cross and an invitation to suffer alongside those who suffer. Leroy Barber is at the forefront of reimagining what missions looks like in the twenty-first century. He helps us see missions not just as something we do with our mouths but something we do with our lives."

SHANE CLAIBORNE, author, activist and recovering sinner, www.thesimpleway.org

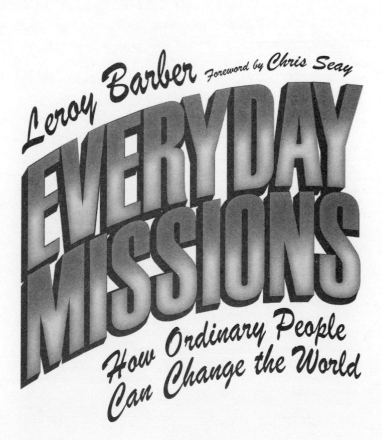

Leroy Barber Foreword by Chris Seay

EVERYDAY MISSIONS

How Ordinary People Can Change the World

IVP Books

An imprint of InterVarsity Press
Downers Grove, Illinois

InterVarsity Press
P.O. Box 1400, Downers Grove, IL 60515-1426
World Wide Web: www.ivpress.com
E-mail: email@ivpress.com

InterVarsity Press® is the book-publishing division of InterVarsity Christian Fellowship/USA®, a
movement of students and faculty active on campus at hundreds of universities, colleges and schools
of nursing in the United States of America, and a member movement of the International Fellowship
of Evangelical Students. For information about local and regional activities, write Public Relations
Dept., InterVarsity Christian Fellowship/USA, 6400 Schroeder Rd., P.O. Box 7895, Madison, WI
53707-7895, or visit the IVCF website at <www.intervarsity.org>.

All Scripture quotations, unless otherwise indicated, are taken from the THE HOLY BIBLE, NEW
INTERNATIONAL VERSION®, NIV® Copyright © 1973, 1978, 1984, 2011 by Biblica, Inc.™ Used
by permission. All rights reserved worldwide.

While all stories in this book are true, names and identifying information in this book have been
changed to protect the privacy of the individuals involved.

The poem on pages 121-22 is written by the author.
The testimonies on pages 92-104 are used by permission.

Design: Cindy Kiple
Images: Toy convertible pulling trailer: Lena Johansson/Glowimages
       Car with trailer: ©Nic Taylor/iStockphoto

ISBN 978-0-8308-3636-9

Printed in the United States of America ∞

Library of Congress Cataloging-in-Publication Data

Barber, Leroy.
  Everyday missions: how ordinary people can change the world / Leroy
Barber.
     p. cm.
  Includes bibliographical references.
  ISBN 978-0-8308-3636-9 (pbk.: alk. paper)
  1. Christian life. I. Title.
  BV4501.3.B364 2012
  248.4—dc23

                                                              2011051585

P	22	21	20	19	18	17	16	15	14	13	12	11	10	9	8	7	6	5	4	3	2	1
Y	30	29	28	27	26	25	24	23	22	21	20	19	18	17	16	15	14	13	12

Contents

Foreword

For most of my life, I was trained to avoid contact with the secular world. We learned that rock and roll music and the failures of our culture could easily lead us astray, and our best shot at becoming faithful Christians was to surround ourselves with those that we considered to be faithful themselves.

It was only from spending time actually reading the Scriptures that I began to discover God's heart for the lowly, for the outcast and for the entire cosmos. God was calling out a people that would be his own to reclaim and redeem all that he created. His strategy for redeeming all things was not based on finding the elite of his day whom he could train and send; he trained them by walking with them. He sent them, as it tells us in the Gospel of Luke, two-by-two with nothing in their wallet and no shoes on their feet. Jesus called them to be the love of God to the people they would encounter.

I have always been confounded by when Jesus taught that we would do greater things than he, after his departure. I read the Gospels with a sense of awe and mystery. I'm astounded to see Jesus feed the five thousand or to call Peter out with him as he walks on the water. I can hardly imagine experiencing even greater things in my own life. As I read the Gospels, it becomes more and more clear that this rag-tag group of disciples that he walked with would begin to tell his story and share his love in a way that results in exponential growth. We would see, as we do today, millions of faithful believers calling people into the love and grace of God.

This book that you're about to read by Leroy Barber is a map into the kind of life you were made to live.

I was recently in Ethiopia working on behalf of my church, Ecclesia Houston, in work that God has called us to do: drill water wells in an area deeply affected by drought. As I spent time sharing coffee with a family living in a small mud hut, I realized that this family had no furniture, no chairs. We sat simply on a dirt floor. The only object they possessed in their home was a small yoke. They had a few donkeys, and they worked the land for their food.

Not many of my friends have a yoke in their garage or among their tools, but yokes were common among the people that Jesus walked with when he taught—as he teaches us in Matthew 11—that all of us who are weary are to come to him, and he will give us rest.

In our culture and day, almost everyone we encounter is tired, over-taxed and seemingly over worked. We live in a place of sleep deprivation, and we long to find rest. When we read this passage and teachings of Jesus our Savior, we discover a sense of hope. I personally wonder if Jesus is going to call me to a day of sleep and rest, or to a spa day where I can become refreshed and ready to begin the work again. But in a surprising twist, Jesus says, "Come to me and I will give you rest. I will put my yoke upon you."

We begin to wonder what Jesus must be talking about. If we're already tired and we need rest, why would he put a yoke upon us that would call us back out to plow the fields?

The truth is, we are not tired and weary because we're doing too much. We're tired and weary because we are busy doing all of the wrong things. We are consumed by the pursuit of wealth, status and possessions that are promising to make our lives better. We are chasing a lie. Our hearts and bodies long to be about the work that we were made to do, serving our King. There's a great harvest waiting in the fields, but as Jesus reminded us, there's a great need for those that will work the harvest.

As you read this book, you will be called into a life as a field worker. For some of you, that seems discouraging; you may, at this point, want to put the book down and move on to something that has more of a self-help trajectory. Let me remind you, however, that you were made to be about this kind of work: loving God and loving people. I believe that you will find in your life, in the same way that I have discovered in my own, that I am at my best, my happiest, my most fulfilled, when I am serving Jesus and living the life of missions every day.

Chris Seay

Introduction

So here's what I want you to do, God helping you: Take your everyday, ordinary life—your sleeping, eating, going-to-work, and walking-around life—and place it before God as an offering. Embracing what God does for you is the best thing you can do for him. Don't become so well adjusted to your culture that you fit into it without even thinking. Instead, fix your attention on God. You'll be changed from the inside out. Readily recognize what he wants from you, and quickly respond to it. Unlike the culture around you, always dragging you down to its level of immaturity, God brings the best out of you, develops well-formed maturity in you.

ROMANS 12:1-2 *The Message*

What is your ordinary life?

Are you sitting in a college classroom, disengaged and unsure of your direction, writing papers on theories that you ache to be living out?

Are you pounding away at a keyboard in your cubicle forty hours a week?

Are you serving coffee and waiting for the next step?

Are you content with your life choices yet still wonder what more God has for you?

Are you living the life everyone encouraged you to pursue and finding it lacking?

If so, you are not alone. Shirin Taber, in her article "Trapped by the Search for Significance," gives us a peek into the mind of young adults.

> I have an insatiable need to feel extraordinary, to be a woman of influence and to leave a mark on the world. . . . Many of my peers—girlfriends, college students and young professionals I have worked among—are feeling the growing itch for significance too. They want to know they matter and that their life has a purpose. They want to help change the world for good, not just watch from the sidelines. I hear it in the way we talk about our dreams and vocational aspirations: "I want to open a shelter for poor and disenfranchised women." "I want to make movies like Steven Spielberg." "I want to be a neuro-surgeon." We believe our God-given destiny is where our greatest happiness lies.[1]

There seems to be, planted in the core of our being, a desire to do something great with our lives, to engage in something that matters—a desperation to be involved in something that connects us to God. We experience the wonder of nature, the handiwork of God in creation, and we acknowledge that God is great, and we discover a desire to do something signifi-cant—to give him every day as an offering. It's like we take in the beauty, love and grace of God, and offer our lives in response. We inhale God, and we exhale significance. By this process we create, but we are also sustained by it; it's fundamental to who we are, and we can't get away from it. The desire to do something extraordinary is created in this process.

Unfortunately, as we search for a place where we feel connected to God in this way, there is a pressure that builds within us. When our work does not satisfy and we endure the drag of a daily grind to pay the bills or the stress of making decisions that won't lead us to a dreary everyday existence. When moving from weekend to weekend or holiday to holiday without much joy or passion in between leads to anger, bitterness, boredom, apathy and laziness. According to a CNN money report:

> Fewer than half of U.S. workers are satisfied with their jobs, the lowest level since record-keeping began 22 years ago. . . . Even though one in 10 Americans is out of a job, those who are employed are increasingly dissatisfied.[2]

In the midst of an economic crisis, you would expect that people would be happy to just be working. But this pervasive job dissatisfaction may simply be the result of a disconnect with significance that people long for in their work; two jobs that consistently top the list as most gratifying, and where people report being the happiest, are "clergy" and "firefighter"—not the highest paying jobs, but jobs that serve people. Taken together—the widespread job dissatisfaction and the type of work that elicits the most happiness—the question seems to be not just "How am I going to get paid?" but "What can I do with my life that brings joy and happiness to myself and others around me?"

The thing is, clergy and firefighters are ordinary people. What they do may sometimes be extraordinary, and their contentment in their work (which is undeniably challenging) may be extraordinary, but they themselves are ordinary people. They wake up, work, interact with strangers and friends and loved ones, deal with challenging relationships and difficult circumstances, eat breakfast, lunch and dinner, and go to bed at night. They're ordinary people; it's what they're doing, and the satisfaction they feel, that gets our attention.

What is your ordinary life? Place it before God as an offering. Embrace what God does for you. Don't become well adjusted to your culture; fix your attention on God. Recognize what he wants from you, and respond to it. No life is too ordinary for God's purposes.

That's easier said than done, of course. Maybe your deepest desire is to live like that, in the center of God's calling, but the specifics feel blurry. It may be that all you feel you have to offer God is your very ordinary life. *You are not alone!* Countless characters in the Bible, as well as faithful servants today, have allowed God to transform their lives from routinely ordinary to powerfully extraordinary for God's glory. Their examples reinforce the truth that no life is too ordinary to accomplish God's purposes. They also demonstrate habits and attitudes that characterize the adventure of extraordinary living.

Consider this scene, reported in all four Gospels: Jesus has gone privately with his followers to a mountainside, but thousands of people have found him. He spends the day teaching them and healing people who were sick. Among the crowd is a small boy. It's not clear why the boy is there; we don't have his name or his background. Maybe he heard the crowd noise and was curious about all the commotion. Maybe he was looking for an adventure and thought what was going on at the mountainside looked promising. Maybe he had heard about this radical teacher and wanted to be near him. The boy could have been there because his parents told him to go and see what was up, or because they brought him along with them—maybe he wished he were somewhere else, playing with his friends.

The boy has food with him. Maybe his mom had thrown a lunch together for him in case it took too long, or perhaps he packed it himself, thinking *This could take a while; I'd better be prepared.* Maybe, even, he stole the lunch from someone along the way. In any case, Jesus is looking for food for all these people, and this boy seems to be the only one there with lunch.

When Christ asked about lunch for the crowd, did this young man quickly and willingly surrender his food? Or did the disciples have to convince him that this was a good thing? Maybe he asked the disciples to ask someone else. Maybe he tried to hide his food because he saw so many hungry people around. Maybe the disciples just took it from him. Had the boy heard of other times when Jesus fed so many from so little and was expecting a miracle? In any case, an ordinary lunch from an ordinary person is either given or taken and eventually winds up in front of Jesus. And Jesus thanks God for it, breaks it up, and feeds thousands of people with it.

This is perhaps our story. For whatever reason and through various ways and attitudes, our ordinary selves wind up in front of Jesus, and a miracle results. Sometimes, against all logic, the extraordinary is manifested, and we are forever changed. Logic would suggest that our small ordinary offerings are totally pointless, but history tells us that small acts have always been the things to change the world. Rosa Parks, for example, was one woman who refused to give her seat to a white man on a race-segregated bus. She did it because she was tired, but not in the way you might think:

> People always say that I didn't give up my seat because I was tired, but that isn't true. I was not tired physically, or no more tired than I usually was at the end of a working day. I was not old, although some people have an image of me as being old then. I was forty-two. No, the only tired I was, was tired of giving in.[3]

That one small thing would become the first small act in a chain of many to change the course of the world.

Even the disciples were skeptical that these five loaves and two small fish that made up that child's lunch could have any significance for a whole crowd of hungry people. Still, Jesus readily accepted the boy's meager offering and multiplied it beyond imagination, providing enough for everyone with food left over. God loves ordinary offerings, and the gift of your life in his hands can make all the difference in the world.

My friend Sean Gladding, in his video series *The Story of God, the Story of Us,* draws our attention to another episode of an ordinary person doing something extraordinary.[4] We enter the story in Mark 12, where Jesus is telling the disciples to observe the crowd giving their money to the temple treasury. A poor widow gives a very small gift, "worth only a few cents" (v. 42). Jesus tells his disciples,

> Truly I tell you, this poor widow has put more into the treasury than all the others. They gave out of their wealth; but she, out of her poverty, put in everything— all she had to live on. (vv. 43-44)

As we look a little deeper into the story, Gladding suggests that Jesus is drawing our attention not to the giving, but to the giver. A person who seemingly has very little to offer her life offers an extraordinary gift that ultimately challenges the entire structure. She is poor, assumed lonely and probably overlooked by most people in the room, but she draws Jesus' attention. He doesn't pity her; he praises her. She isn't devalued by Jesus but is lifted up as an example. More important, Jesus confronts the culture that overlooks her; perhaps she wouldn't be suffering in poverty if others in the temple would pay attention. She had nothing left after this offering; perhaps Jesus was giving the disciples a heads up to care for her and others like her.

Jesus welcomes our ordinary offerings because it's the ordinary things that best teach about faith and sacrifice. It's also the ordinary things that point out the holes in our society—the things that should not be accepted as normal. Ordinary offerings do not go unnoticed by God; in fact, God can use ordinary offerings to change the world.

God wants all of your ordinary life—your sleeping, eating, going-to-work and walking-around life—as an offering. When you choose to give it, God will transform your time, talents, and experience to use them for incredible, God-honoring, extraordinary purposes.

I felt compelled to write this book for several reasons. First of all, in my work with Mission Year, the urban ministry that I lead, I have the opportunity to interact with young adults all across the country. I see these young people bursting with potential and able to serve God in extraordinary ways. However, I am often saddened by a sense that many of these young adults do not see themselves as having anything to offer God. Often they have lost faith in the church and may be losing faith in God as well. A 2006 Barna study suggests that church attendance for young adults is way down.[5] The Higher Education Research Institute at UCLA found that frequent church attendance among college students dropped from 52 percent the year before entering college to only 29 percent by junior year.[6]

There is also at the same time a growing tendency among young people to make commitments to serve out of their commitment to faith—as evidenced by the popularity of programs like Mission Year, Teach for America, Americorps and others. I think such organizations encourage and inspire young people by pointing them to the extraordinary purposes God has for them: he has equipped each individual to accomplish their calling and declared that he is sufficient in their weaknesses. I am excited to see how the Lord moves when young people of God step out in faith and trust him to accomplish his good work in their lives. Still, what I often see instead are young adults locked into activities that are off the mark from their deeper calling. They seem to be killing time.

I cannot count how many times people have expressed to me that they are not just unhappy with their present circumstances, but they actually don't believe that what they are doing is really what they *should* be doing.

- Brian, a college senior only months away from graduation, walks up to me and declares, "I don't know where I am going next, because my degree is in something that I am not interested in."

- Mark, a businessman, tells me that he hates his work and only does it to pay the bills, but most days he is miserable.

- Kayla says that she really wants to serve among the urban poor with Mission Year, but she can't because her parents won't understand.

There is a link here between doing something you don't enjoy and living out an extraordinary call. Paul's suggestion in Romans 12 to turn over your ordinary self could, for people in this circumstance, be a path of transformation. That path begins when we offer God our everyday selves—even if we think that self is disappointing or mundane. The offering pleases God, which gives us the courage to live differently—not according to the pattern of this world. This is a sign of a renewed mind that links us to God's ways and will. Christ has a calling on each life that is simply waiting to be lived, but I don't think we get there until we make that ordinary, everyday offering.

1

Start Running

I was a rather ordinary student when I entered the fairly large Temple University in Philadelphia at eighteen years old. I had average grades—a solid C student. And I had been active in high school as an athlete (football and track), but I didn't come to Temple on any scholarships. I ended high school feeling comfortable, but generally under the radar and significantly ordinary.

When I was considering my direction and a future, I asked several questions:

- What would prepare me for a good job?
- What job would pay well?
- What will help me survive?
- What will be the easiest courses for me to take?
- What would be safe?
- What work would not hinder my fun?

I declared my major as accounting. I had taken one class in high school, and it seemed to come easily to me, and I liked solving problems, so it seemed like a perfect fit. Those who know me today burst out laughing at the thought of me as an accountant—it is completely the opposite of who I am as a person—but at the time I could see myself sitting in an office, balancing the books, and then heading home in the evenings to take in a Phillies game. These were not bad things I was dreaming for myself, but they had little do to with calling and more to do with comfort—an imagined reality to make up for the hardship I had endured in life up to that point. But reality kicked in soon enough, as I realized I was not cut out for accounting. I was sitting in my Managerial Accounting classroom, devastated because I could not catch on. I even met with a tutor, but nothing helped.

As I struggled to get through this class, my future fantasies became blurry. *What is happening to me?* I thought. *Why is this so hard?* Tears, disappointment and eventually failure followed. I began to skip class and play video games at the student center instead, which led to failing grades and eventually academic probation. I kept it a secret from my mom—she didn't see the grades, and there was no phone call home from college when you missed class, no teacher looking for you. The slide got worse and worse. *What was I to do now, God?*

As I reviewed my life, I realized that God was somewhere on the periphery; I was at the center. I acknowledged God but was not totally open to his plan for my life. The question *Who am I?* lingered in my mind. I needed to do something; more to the point, I needed God to do something for me. I needed to turn over my ordinary life to God and let him make something of it.

God has created us for more than we can imagine. We have limited vision—we see stuff we want, stuff we're afraid of, stuff that makes us uncomfortable, stuff that obstructs our vision of what could be, what should be. That's why we need to give our selves to God—he has a better line of sight. In this book I want us to walk together to discover how God uses ordinary lives for his extraordinary purposes. I am excited to listen together to the stories of saints—those in the Bible and those on today's streets—who can teach us about how God transformed their lives. We will join with the writer of Hebrews:

> Do you see what this means—all these pioneers who blazed the way, all these veterans cheering us on? It means we'd better get on with it. Strip down, start running—and never quit! No extra spiritual fat, no parasitic sins. Keep your eyes on *Jesus,* who both began and finished this race we're in. (Hebrews 12:1-2 *The Message*)

I know it may seem like a long way for some to go from where you're sitting—your desk or dorm room, your cubicle or kitchen—to a dynamic race like this one, where you are energized and committed for your run. You may be reading on a lunch break in a locker room and can't see a connection. You may be working the graveyard shift dumping trash cans and cannot be convinced to start running. On the television show *The Office,* regional manager Michael Scott takes the entire staff through "safety training," but is talked into a depression when his worklife is compared to the work that goes on in the warehouse: "This [office work] is shenanigans, foolishness. Nerf ball. You live a sweet little Nerfy life. Sittin' on your biscuit. Never having to risk it. . . . It takes courage just to be you." How much does it take for you to be you?

Maybe you read Paul's words to the Corinthians and don't want to run the same risk:

> I've worked much harder, been jailed more often, beaten up more times than I can count, and at death's door time after time. I've been flogged five times with the Jews' thirty-nine lashes, beaten by Roman rods three times, pummeled with rocks once. I've been ship-wrecked three times, and immersed in the open sea for a night and a day. In hard traveling year in and year out, I've had to ford rivers, fend off robbers, struggle with friends, struggle with foes. I've been at risk in the city, at risk in the country, endangered by desert sun and sea storm, and betrayed by those I thought were my broth-ers. I've known drudgery and hard labor, many a long and lonely night without sleep, many a missed meal, blasted by the cold, naked to the weather. (2 Corinthi-ans 11:23-27 *The Message*)

The life of faith Paul describes does not come easy and is not without its share of struggles, but neither is an everyday life. We have to make decisions about money, family and life every day; it gets particularly dicey when we look at those things through the lens of the gospel. But the rewards of the journey Paul describes for us are incredible, and I am eager to share stories with you that may inspire you to start run-ning and never quit!

I was once visiting Mission Year volunteers in Buenos Aires, Argentina, when they invited me to come along to the Fatima community where they were serving. Buenos Aires is the capital and largest city of Argentina, and the third-largest metropolitan area in South America, with a population of around thirteen million. Each time I visit the downtown area of Buenos Aries, with its large billboards advertising everything from cell phones to underwear, I get the feeling I am in New York City. Strongly influenced by European culture, Buenos Aires is sometimes referred to as the "Paris of South America." The city has the busiest legitimate industry in Latin America, with scores of theaters and productions. Buenos Aires is the site of the Teatro Colón, an internationally rated opera house. There are several symphony orchestras and choral societies. The city has numerous museums related to history, fine arts, modern arts, decorative arts, popular arts, sacred art, arts and crafts, theater and popular music, as well as the preserved homes of noted art collectors, writers, composers and artists. The city is home to hundreds of bookstores, public libraries and cultural associations (it is sometimes called "the city of books"), as well as the largest concentration of active theaters in Latin America. It has a world-famous zoo and botanical garden, a large number of landscaped parks and squares, as well as churches and places of worship of many denominations, many of which are architecturally noteworthy.

Buenos Aires attracts migrants from Argentina's provinces and neighboring countries. Shanty towns (*villas miseria*) started growing around the city's industrial areas during the

1930s, leading to pervasive social problems and social contrasts with the largely upwardly mobile Buenos Aires population. These neighborhoods are very different from the tourist areas in the downtown, but in the center of one of the poorest, most dangerous places you can imagine, I am challenged by a graciousness that surpasses even the famous southern hospitality of my Atlanta home.

I had become accustomed to the elegant restaurants, international shopping venues, salesmen offering trademark Argentine leather products and young men promoting Tango lessons to tourists that make up Buenos Aries. But Fatima, where my Mission Year friends serve, is different. The manicured medians of Buenos Aries are replaced in Fatima with piles of trash down the center of roads. Men hunt through the refuse seeking items to recycle for money. Neglected dogs roam the streets. Dwellings with crumbling cinderblock walls and dirt floors—buildings that would not pass a single building code in the United States—house the neighborhood residents. Fatima is notorious for its poverty and violence, and locals will warn you away from its geographic boundaries. What's true in Buenos Aries is true everywhere: where there is great wealth, there is also great poverty.

But I cannot bypass an opportunity to share a meal with my brothers and sisters, so off to Fatima we went. Juan, a Fatima resident, uses a white diesel flat bed truck to transport teams of volunteers to their service sites; on this day he arrived to carry us to his house. When Juan and Marcheeta saw kids in their community without a safe space, Juan built an extra room in their home to serve as a community center. Neighborhood children come there regularly now for afterschool programs, meals and Bible study. I jumped in the front seat with Juan, a slender, older gentleman with a strong face. When we arrived at his simple home, I saw basic floors, four rooms and a kitchen. The windows in his home have no glass, but bright, colorful materials serve as curtains. Mismatched tables are pushed together to create space for guests, and a mix of plastic and wooden chairs surround the table, which now nearly fills the room. Juan lives with his wife and children, most of whom are now adults themselves. As we entered Juan's home, each new visitor headed straight for his wife, Marcheeta, and greeted her with a customary kiss on both cheeks. She sat at the center of the cloth-covered table, enjoying her matriarch status and directing preparations for the feast. *Asada* (grilled steak) was cooked to perfection and adorned by salad and break. Marcheeta assigned seats to the guests, drinks were poured, and we joined together over a meal of laughter, delicious food, rapid conversation and fast translation.

This is Fatima, and Juan and Marcheeta's house is the center of the Fatima neighborhood. It is extraordinary. Juan and Marcheeta are living extraordinary lives. Their lack of money, power, education or any other resource are not a barrier to them. This family may not possess the world's requirements for greatness, but God knows no bounds with lives that are submitted to his leading.

This journey into the extraordinary life is open to all of us because the prerequisites—hospitality, love, genuine openness and generosity—are available to all of us, regardless of what value the world places on what we have to offer. Juan and Marcheeta have presented their concrete home, home-made curtains and mismatched chairs all to the glory of God. God has transformed their offering into a safe space for beloved children and neighbors and an example of the true hospitability of God's people.

Reflecting on the lives of everyday people I encounter, such as Juan and Macheeta, who are doing great things for the glory of God—as well as examining the inspiring leaders in the Word of God—I notice some common themes. The questions that drive the thought processes of people who have submitted their ordinary lives to God's extraordinary purposes differ significantly from the ones I listed for myself when I was entering college. Our ordinary lives can begin to look vastly different when we ask different questions. Instead of focusing on the mandate "I need to have a job," a person who is starting to experience God's extraordinary plan for them is asking vocational questions: "What am I good at?" she asks. "How has God made me? What brings me joy?" These questions lead in vastly different directions than "What pays well? What will cover all my bills? What will not hinder my time for fun?"

There are other areas of difference, too. Ordinary lives place an inordinate value on safety and abhor the idea of risk. We are a society that protects ourselves wherever we can, whether it's avoiding bad parts of town or securing our homes with multiple alarm systems. How are we supposed to turn ourselves completely over to God so he can transform our lives when we've invested so much of ourselves in invulnerability?

There is Scripture, of course, that tells us to count the cost. But counting the cost is not an excuse for avoiding the challenges of an extraordinary life. This count is so we are aware of the risk, not so we have an excuse for avoidance. There are people in unsafe places in need of God's extraordinary power, and God needs an offering to go to work in those places. There are children who are being trafficked for sex in some of the nastiest places we could imagine, there are schools in challenging neighborhoods that need good teachers to come in and teach, there are men, women and children living on benches without food. Lives offered for God's use are willing to take risks, recognizing at every turn that God is in control. The ordinary life fears "rocking the boat" or doing anything out of their ordinary standard. But lives offered for God's use seek out new and unique ideas. They value all gifts and talents and what someone else might bring to the table.

Dreams reveal much about the path on which a person is journeying. Some dream only of themselves: "How am I going to retire? Where will I live and how will I pass my leisure time? What do I need to do now to make that dream a reality?" Others' dreams reach a little wider. They want to see their community restored. They desire to see peace, joy, health and beauty prosper. They ask together, "How can we change the world?"

What is the role of money in your life? Ordinary thinkers see money as the means and the end. You earn so that you possess more money. You obtain financial security. The extraordinary thinker sees money as a means to accomplish much bigger goals. There are selfless plans—directions guided by God—that motivate this person. Money is simply the resource needed to continue the work for God's kingdom.

One final difference I have observed between ordinary and extraordinary lives is the use of time. Televisions, video games, movies and other forms of entertainment take a lot of time in the ordinary life. While none of these leisure activities may be bad within themselves, a person who consumes entertainment at a never-ending pace is missing out on something greater. The need to be entertained is rarely satisfied. Lives submitted to extraordinary purposes are constant learners who invest time developing and nurturing new skills and interests. They love to teach others new things.

Time, money, dreams, risk—negotiating these aspects of the ordinary life is quite a challenge, but God is facing the challenge for us. We are ordinary people offering ourselves to the possibility that God will do great things through us. Where are you at this moment? Is your heart longing to be near God and seeing him work extraordinarily around your life? Are you engaged in something you truly want to do? Or are you settling for something less? Are you actually running from someone or some situation? Are you living in a place where you do not belong? Are you spiritually "stuck"? Even today, have you already said yes to something you did not want to say yes to? Have your simple choices led you to live life differently than you imagined it?

God is asking for your ordinary life—your sleeping, eating, going-to-work, walking-around life. Ordinary people infused with God's extraordinary purposes absolutely can change the world. This collection of characteristics I've noted is certainly not exhaustive, but will serve as the basis for our journey together. I want to look at each thought process more intentionally and highlight biblical examples of ordinary people who did extraordinary things. Meet average people called by God to live stories of greatness. I will also share examples in today's society that teach us how to incorporate more extraordinary thinking into our lives. You have an open invitation to join these God-inspired efforts to change the world through your simple offerings to Christ.

2

The Myth of Extraordinary

Who wouldn't want to be extraordinary? Most people gravitate toward the idea that we can be exceptional. Parents, teachers and coaches challenge us to be the best we can be, to step outside of the norm, to do everything with excellence. These notions are great for our spirit and in many cases encourage us throughout life. The problem that occurs, in many cases, is that a spirit of elitism can develop disguised in the name of excellence. Egotism, vanity, conceit and plain selfishness emerge.

When we're regularly being challenged to be extraordinary, the idea of being ordinary can start to sound like mediocrity. Nobody is proud of a C grade point average, even though a C is meant to denote an average performance. President George W. Bush even joked about his own average school performance at a commencement address at Yale: "To those of you who received honors, awards and distinctions, I say well done. And to the C students, I say: You, too, can be president of the United States."[7] But outside of school, a C grade might as well be an F. Ordinary is not what most of us shoot for as a goal. In fact most probably shy away from idea of being regular, common or run of the mill. Ordinary can been seen as a negative and therefore move people into thoughts of failure and even breakdown.

THE MJ SYNDROME

With very few exceptions, fans of professional basketball consider Michael Jordan the greatest player to ever play the game. Jordan's individual accolades and accomplishments include five MVP awards, ten All-NBA First Team designations, nine All-Defensive First Team honors, fourteen NBA All-Star Game appearances, three All-Star Game MVP awards, ten scoring titles, three steals titles, six NBA Finals MVP awards, and the 1988 NBA Defensive Player of the Year award. He holds the NBA records for highest career regular season scoring average (30.12 points per game) and highest career playoff scoring average (33.45 points per game). During his career he led his team to six NBA titles. In 1999, ESPN named him the greatest North American athlete of the twentieth century, and the Associated Press listed him second only to Babe Ruth on its list of athletes of the century. He was inducted to the Basketball Hall of Fame in 2009. Jordan is now the measure of every basketball player to enter the league, and while there are many great players that have come after him, with Jordan as the standard many players will likely be remembered as average or even failures. Michael Jordan has earned an elite status, and there's little room around him for other players.

Contrast Michael Jordan with Manute Bol. Bol played basketball for many teams over his career—two colleges and four NBA teams. He was known as a specialist player; his shot blocking skills were considered among the best in the history of the sport. But other aspects of his game were considered fairly weak. He is, for example, the only player in NBA history to have more blocked shots than points scored, having blocked 2,086 shots and scored only 1,599 points. Over the course of his ten-year career, Bol averaged 2.6 points, 4.2 rebounds, 0.3 assists and 3.3 blocks per game while only playing an average of 18.7 minutes per game. Having appeared in 624 games over ten seasons, as of 2010 Manute Bol remained

- first in career blocks per 48 minutes (8.6), far ahead of second-place Mark Eaton (5.8)

- second in career blocks-per-game average (3.34)

- fourteenth in total blocked shots (2,086)

And yet compared to Michael Jordan, who played in the NBA at the same time and also had a ten-year career, Manute Bol was an average player. When we compare ordinary to extraordinary we end up with these two extremes: elite or failure.

"Elite" is a category that helps us designate people who are, effectively, in a class by themselves. To be called elite is to be credited with a significant accomplishment, something that ordinary people rarely accomplish. Elitism is something different, more problematic. Elitism is a way of viewing the world around you, a way of acting in the world, that assumes you are better than everyone else. Elitism is essentially a superiority complex.

Elitism separates us from one another and promotes artificial boundaries and unfair judgments against each other. Elitism can cause great pain. The idea that certain people are just better than other people has led to discrimination and war, even slavery and holocaust. But even smaller manifestations of elitism, such as cliques and clubs, can cause immense pain and devastating consequences.

Our human tendency to label and create categories hinders our connection with God. When we compare ourselves to each other we look for failures and limitations; when we compare ourselves to God and his work we realize that we are all quite ordinary. That doesn't mean we are all doomed to failure, but we must contend with the human limitations in our behavior and lifestyles. Our task is to rid ourselves of elitism In reality, God doesn't have a category for "elite." As it is written:

> There is no one righteous, not even one;
>   there is no one who understands;
>   there is no one who seeks God.
> All have turned away,
>   they have together become worthless;
> there is no one who does good,
>   not even one. (Romans 3:10-12)

Measured against God, everyone falls short. And yet God doesn't disqualify people from his work for falling short. In fact, God seems to revel in working through people who fall short—not only of God's standards but of the world's measures of greatness.

> Brothers and sisters, think of what you were when you were called. Not many of you were wise by human standards; not many were influential; not many were of noble birth. But God chose the foolish things of the world to shame the wise; God chose the weak things of the world to shame the strong. God chose the lowly things of this world and the despised things—and the things that are not—to nullify the things that are. (1 Corinthians 1:26-28)

God as our Creator is saying to us, "I will take the things you think are meaningless in your life and use those to do incredible things." We are not called to elitism or to mediocrity; we are called to join God's plan. That plan starts with the realization that the extraordinary one is God. He is the beginning and end of all things. When we concede greatness to God, we benefit from his astonishing work, which makes us all significant.

When I first started working for Mission Year I was the city director in Atlanta. Part of the work of a city director is to meet once a month with each team member who is serving in that city for the year. We call them "one-on-ones." Tom came to Mission Year as a college graduate and had many accolades from his professors and peers. I remember reading his application, and it was loaded with phrases like "good leader," "self-starter" and "great communicator." There were various awards of excellence listed, and as I read Tom's application I thought, *How cool that he is going to serve this year.* When Tom arrived, it was just as expected: he was very smart, an incredible communicator and very well versed in Scripture. But at our first one-on-one, Tom pretty much told me how things should be run. He had done this before, he let me know, and he offered himself to me in case I needed any help. Tom was a good person and knew it; he was sure he knew how to help the people of the "inner city," even though he had never lived, worked or had a relationship with anyone from the "inner city." He saw himself as better than most who lived in the neighborhood where he was serving. Tom's ego was as big as they come.

I received complaints about Tom's attitude from the agency where he served and from his team members, who lived with him through the year. Tom was turning out to be a nightmare.

Mary's application to Mission Year was similarly full of good things she had done in college. She had experience working with a local after-school program, spending time helping in chapel and mentoring a young girl from the local school. Mary was primed for Mission Year; she had gone on a mission trip to the city during her sophomore year and was instantly hooked. Her application was full of words like "good spirit," "servant" and "team player." I thought as I read her application, *This is perfect! She will be great for our program. I can't wait to meet her.*

My first one-on-one with Mary was interesting. She felt incredibly overwhelmed and could not see herself making it through the first week, let alone the year. She cried for most of the hour, and it took a lot of convincing for her not to leave the next day. Mary's one-on-ones were quite draining as I spent most of the time encouraging her to stay and consoling her through tears. We would go back and forth in her one-on-ones, with her crying and saying, "I can't do this," and me encouraging her that she could.

Sometime in our February or March one-on-ones, both Tom and Mary came to breaking points. Tom could not understand why things had not changed on his block, despite his great Bible studies and wonderful outreach. Mary was not feeling adequate at all and was ready to go home right away. The magical moment happened for both of them as they decided they needed to stop concentrating on themselves. Their human understanding and strength was spent, so they both decided to just show up everyday and let God handle the situation. Tom declared, "I am tired. If God wants to do something, then I will have to watch him do it. My ways aren't working." Mary proclaimed, "If God wants to use my untalented self, then I will let him." That moment when they completely put themselves in God's hand turned out to be just the thing. They both finished the year well, and the one-on-ones got much better. (Thank God!)

> For God, who said, "Let light shine out of darkness," made his light shine in our hearts to give us the light of the knowledge of God's glory displayed in the face of Christ. But we have this treasure in jars of clay to show that this all-surpassing power is from God and not from us. (2 Corinthians 4:6-7)

Any good thing done is done by God, and any person

called is called by God, and any gift or talent is given by God to accomplish his purposes in the world. Strength to do or not do is all power given by God. The idea that any of us is extraordinary is a myth.

On the eve of his crucifixion Jesus has this conversation with Pontius Pilate. Pilate declares that he has the power to save Jesus, but Jesus replies, "You have no power except that which has been given to you from my Father." May the extraordinary God give you the strength to trust him to turn your whole self over to him—the things about yourself that you're most proud of, and those things that make you feel inadequate. May the God who holds all power reveal himself to you in a way that guards you from elitism and inspires more than mediocrity from you, a way that brings hope, restoration and peace to and through your ordinary life.

3

Kingdom Imagination

MOSES'S STORY

We are not defined by our careers or our relationships or even our life's passions. God's ultimate and immediate will for our lives as believers becomes simply this: That we would pursue Him every single day of our lives. That is what defines us.

BEBO NORMAN

Moses sent spies to the Promised Land to check things out. They brought back a mixed report.

They gave Moses this account: "We went into the land to which you sent us, and it does flow with milk and honey! Here is its fruit. But the people who live there are powerful, and the cities are fortified and very large. We even saw descendants of Anak there. The Amalekites live in the Negev; the Hittites, Jebusites and Amorites live in the hill country; and the Canaanites live near the sea and along the Jordan."

Then Caleb silenced the people before Moses and said, "We should go up and take possession of the land, for we can certainly do it."

But the men who had gone up with him said, "We can't attack those people; they are stronger than we are." And they spread among the Israelites a bad report about the land they had explored. They said, "The land we explored devours those living in it. All the people we saw there are of great size. We saw the Nephilim there (the descendants of Anak come from the Nephilim). We seemed like grasshoppers in our own eyes, and we looked the same to them." (Numbers 13:27-33)

There was a consensus from the spies that the land was indeed wonderful and flowed with milk and honey. They spies even brought back samples to show Moses and the people some proof. But from there the reports differed. Eight of the spies began to talk about the giants that inhabited the land and the walls that fortified the cities; they gave the report that they could not take this land. Caleb and Joshua, on the other hand, thought God could and would give the land to them. The reports differed based on something I call *kingdom imagination.*

Kingdom imagination combines a few key things to create an outlook based on God's supernatural involvement. First it takes into account the past, where God has been present in past circumstances. Kingdom imagination first considers specific places and situations where God did something miraculous. He may have healed a sick person, provided finances, diminished or deleted an obstacle. Whatever the case, it is a time or place where we know it was God. What has he done before that can be counted on in the present? Some call this a testimony or praise report.

That instance for Joshua and Caleb could have been the manna falling from heaven or the fire leading them by night on the exodus from Egypt. Either of these (or various other experiences of God's care and concern) could serve as proof that God was indeed able to do something amazing. Whatever it was for Caleb and Joshua, the other spies left that level of praise out of their report.

Kingdom imagination also sees past present circumstances. Kingdom imagination is able to see possibility in the midst of present obstacles, hope through despair. It relies on the vast resources of God and speaks boldly of future reality as if it were present. The kingdom imagination is not arrogant but bold—bold enough to speak openly about things that haven't happened yet. Caleb quiets the crowd and declares, "We can take this land." Caleb is just not a crazy or naïve person here; he is, rather, a bold follower of God, and his kingdom imagination gives him the courage to speak out what he believes God can do. He speaks it, and he stands by it—even though he is in the minority. He doesn't hold merely a minority opinion, however; Caleb isn't debating the readiness of the Israelites but rather acknowledging the power of God. Kingdom imagination isn't a matter of debate; it's a point of view.

Caleb's view, as we witness in Scripture, was not one the people of Israel acted on, and so it is with kingdom imagination. It is a bold view and a prediction that sometimes take years upon years to materialize. But whether it is realized in the short term or far into the future, kingdom imagination is usually present in the extraordinary work of God.

Loving God. Loving people. These are the motivations of those inspired by a kingdom imagination. Others may look at their lives and commend them, but loving God and loving people are not always compatible with the "American dream." People who act on a kingdom imagination might be mocked or excluded; they might even be hated by whole groups of people. But that's irrelevant to them, just as Israel's rejection of their report was irrelevant to Caleb and Joshua.

The drivers of popular society—fame, wealth, attention and the praise—have no place in a kingdom imagination, and they cannot sustain the challenges that may cross your path while following Christ with abandon. Any motivations short of seeking to honor God and serve others in everything you do will not sustain such a journey.

Those living God-inspired lives are in no way super-human, and their lives may lack glamour. They make mistakes, but they admit them and seek restoration. That's because they've encountered God, been inspired with a kingdom imagination, and had their view of the world changed as a result.

Encounters with God deepen our commitment to love him and love others. Those experiences by which we come to know him and are moved to action vary with each person's story. The Bible is full of men and women who find themselves swept into a story bigger than the one they were living—everyday people being transformed in the context of their ordinary lives. Their inspired encounters reveal the unique ways that God can choose to move in our daily lives. Though not exhaustive, their stories may remind you of moments where God has called you and equipped you for something more than the life you are living. Our responses to those encounters make the difference between ordinary and extraordinary.

OVERWHELMED BY GOD: MOSES'S STORY

Moses's life started off on a less-than-usual note. A Hebrew baby, Moses was born during a time when Egypt's Pharaoh was killing Hebrew boys in hopes of protecting his throne from the people he was keeping in slavery. In desperate response, Moses's mother hid him after birth and sent him floating down a river. Pharaoh's daughter discovered him and raised him as an Egyptian ruler.

This position was certainly one society would deem extraordinary. But Moses later learned of his true identity, a child of the oppressed; and eventually when he witnessed an Egyptian beating a Hebrew, he killed the Egyptian and fled to avoid punishment. Moses found himself in exile, wandering in search of his next step.

He ended up at a well in Midian when he witnessed some shepherds hassling a group of women—and not just any women, but the daughters of the priest of Midian. Moses stepped in to stand up for the women and was invited to dinner out of gratitude from their father, Jethro. Moses accepted Jethro's invitation and eventually married one of his daughters.

Moses begins filling the expected roles of young man—

husband, father, son-in-law, farmer. Living with and working for his father-in-law, Moses's life is good. But it is not all that God has planned for him.

Scripture tells of Moses working outside, tending the sheep his father-in-law owns. In this everyday moment, God chooses to overwhelm Moses with his presence. A bush is burning, which isn't all that unusual; I am sure that, being in the middle of the desert, Moses has seen bushes burning before. There may even have been other bushes burning at the same time as this one. But this one drew his attention. Why on this particular day did this one draw him in? What was different about this particular bush burning?

In the middle of Moses's routine, something sticks out and captures his attention. Days and times happen like this, and we cannot explain why we were drawn in or justify the time it takes to investigate. But we gaze anyway, and sometimes it is in this gaze that we see something odd or new and we walk toward it.

Investigating requires some time and energy. Once he decides to investigate, Moses has to climb up to this bush to check out the scene. He leaves his duties; he abandons his routine. The bush is on fire but is not consumed. How is that possible? Is this really a fire? Something unnatural is happening, and it draws Moses in even more. Maybe he is concerned for keeping the sheep safe. Maybe he's curious; something on fire should burn up. That only makes good sense. What in the world is going on up there?

As Moses gets close, God calls his name from the bush. This is the part of the story that gives me chills. What started out as an ordinary day is now transformed into a life-changing experience. This is the call—the moment when you realize God has chosen you for some work. The moment is surreal, unlike nothing you have experienced before. It can bring tears, fear, relief or dismay. Some people experience one or all of these emotions at once. It can pass quickly or go on for days at a time. One thing for sure, you realize—one way or another, whether it's dramatic or in the quietness of your heart—that it's you and God in this moment, and there's no way around it.

"Do not come any closer," God said. "Take off your sandals, for the place where you are standing is holy ground." Then he said, "I am the God of your father, the God of Abraham, the God of Isaac and the God of Jacob." At this, Moses hid his face, because he was afraid to look at God.

The LORD said, "I have indeed seen the misery of my people in Egypt. I have heard them crying out because of their slave drivers, and I am concerned about their suffering. So I have come down to rescue them from the hand of the Egyptians and to bring them up out of that land into a good and spacious land, a land flowing with milk and honey—the home of the Canaanites, Hittites, Amorites, Perizzites, Hivites and Jebusites. And now the cry of the Israelites has reached me, and I have seen the way the Egyptians are oppressing them. So now, go. I am sending you to Pharaoh to bring my people the Israelites out of Egypt." (Exodus 3:5-10)

During this time that Moses has been walking through his days, God has been orchestrating a kingdom story in which Moses would one day play a part. The pharaoh who had chased Moses out of Egypt is now dead, the slavery of the Israelites has become more oppressive, and God will not let their cries go without response.

Moses, of course, has questions. *Who am I? How can I be expected to approach Pharaoh? What will I even say?* God simply encourages Moses: "I am with you. Tell him I am that I am."

What a change from tending the sheep the day before! God's plan may not always jibe with our "sensibilities," but an overwhelming experience with the Divine transcends our concerns and inspires our response. We must jump up! We must respond! We must act! A consuming encounter of this kind can produce an instant change in one's life. Moses immediately sets out for Egypt to free the Israelites. When some people transform overnight from ordinary to extraordinary, they do not need others' permission or convincing. They have experienced God's clear calling, and though they may have questions, they trust that God is who he says he is, and he will not leave.

I can identify with this in some way. When my wife, Donna, and I felt very clearly the Lord tell us to pack up our family in Philadelphia and move, our whole family visited Atlanta, Georgia, to meet with Bob Lupton, the president and founder of what was then Family Consultation Services Urban Ministries. Many times I'd stated, "I will never live in the South. I am a proud to be a Philadelphian." Philly was hard and had its problems, but it was my city and I was proud of it. But God has a way of changing your plans.

There were children growing up in Atlanta who didn't have many educational choices. Bob wanted to expand their options by starting a new school. Cornerstone, where we were working in Philly, had been started for the same purpose, but nevertheless we didn't feel at all qualified to begin this work in Atlanta. But we felt God moving us in this direction.

Bob showed us around the city. He'd begun working with families in the Atlanta area in the mid-1970s. Over the years, Bob's ministry had developed into a community development organization that provided housing, job training and jobs. He drove us by a house in Eastlake and said, "FCS is going to purchase that house and it will be available for a family in ministry." It was currently being used as a crack house, he admitted, and living in the vicinity might pose some challenges. But that news didn't discourage me; as soon as we'd driven into the neighborhood, God put it on my heart that this was where he wanted us. Donna squeezed my hand and I knew she felt the same way.

"That'll be perfect," I said. I was pleased by the large yard and driveway. The house seemed like a blessing after our years of living in a Philly row house—a small, two-story home with no front yard. Our front steps opened up to the sidewalk. Row houses share walls with the houses on either side, so we could hear our neighbors going up and down stairs, and if they talked too loud, you could hear what they were saying. Usually row houses had basements and a flat roof. They were about sixteen feet wide, and sixty to seventy-five feet long. There were many blocks of these houses, fifty to sixty on a block. The streets were narrow with room for parking on one side only. Often we'd have to wait for people to move their car to be able to park ours.

Of course we prayed about our decision. We were encouraged to proceed when we read and reflected on Joshua 1:1-9. After the death of Moses, God spoke to Joshua and told him to cross the Jordan River and go to the country God was giving the people of Israel. God promised that he would be with Joshua just as he was with Moses. God wouldn't give up on Joshua, nor would he leave him. God told Joshua to give it all he had, including his heart and soul. He was to have strength and courage, not to be timid or discouraged; God would be with him every step of the way.

I knew God's promise to Joshua was for me too. Donna and I felt the Lord pulling us toward Atlanta, and it was time we answered God's call. We brought our three young children and only a few things to a place about which we knew nearly nothing.

We are a family who enjoys road trips, but this was different from any of those experiences. While we knew the city where we would stop driving, our true destination was not clear. *Why us, God? Why Atlanta? Why now? How will we provide for our kids? Will they make friends and be accepted? Have we hurt them by making such a big change?* We knew no one in Atlanta. We had very little money. Our kids were three, six and nine years old; We were thirty-one and thirty-two years old, and eleven years into a marriage. We had no idea how things would work out. All we knew was that we were answering God's call, and that he had promised he was with us.

Do you know beyond a shadow of doubt that God has called you? You cannot explain why or answer all the questions the stem from that calling; still, you have encountered God so powerfully that you absolutely know you must respond? You have seen a bush burning without being consumed and heard your name shouted or whispered and you cannot deny it? You may be in the midst of a transformative call out of the ordinary and into the extraordinary. May the God of peace, who called Moses out of a sheep-tending life into a slave-freeing mission, be present with you. May he give you a kingdom imagination and the strength and courage to go with it. May he calm your spirit and give you hope in the assurance that God has sent you, and he *will* be with you always.

4

God-Confidence

DAVID'S STORY

There are two kinds of confidence. The more common kind of confidence, the one we most often aspire to, is self-confidence. Self-confidence has mostly to do with self-perception. The website "Pick the Brain" offers ten ways to build self-confidence. Here are some of those recommendations:

1. *Dress sharp.* "When you don't look good, it changes the way you carry yourself and interact with other people. . . . In most cases, significant improvements can be made by bathing and shaving frequently, wearing clean clothes, and being cognizant of the latest styles."

2. *Walk faster.* "One of the easiest ways to tell how a person feels about herself is to examine her walk. Is it slow? tired? painful? Or is it energetic and purposeful? People with confidence walk quickly."

3. *Good posture.* "By practicing good posture, you'll automatically feel more confident. Stand up straight, keep your head up, and make eye contact. You'll make a positive im-

pression on others and instantly feel more alert and empowered."

4. *Personal commercial.* "Write a 30-60 second speech that highlights your strengths and goals. Then recite it in front of the mirror aloud (or inside your head if you prefer) whenever you need a confidence boost." . . .

5. *Sit in the front row.* "By deciding to sit in the front row, you can . . . build your self confidence. You'll also be more visible to the important people talking from the front of the room."[8]

There is nothing wrong with the practices suggested by Pick the Brain, and they probably would make a person seem more confident. We see a different kind of confidence, however, when we observe people who we see in the Scriptures taken by a kingdom imagination. The confidence displayed by David, for example, seems to go a lot deeper than the perceived confidence championed by Pick the Brain.

God-confidence comes from the practice of letting each experience of God build on the one previous. Donald Miller writes in his blog "How to Get Confidence from God":

The Christian faith is a practical faith. God employs experience in order to teach us, to develop our abilities. And even then, He is more interested in the interaction He has with us in the process than He is in teaching us anything at all. God is not our boss, He is our Father. The whole world is an educational playground God is using to bring you toward perfection, to raise you as His own child.

If we believe God is a genie with a wand granting wishes and doing magic tricks, we don't understand the God of the Bible.

God gave David confidence keeping lions from his sheep, then killing Goliath, then running a country, God did not give David a country and then instill in him magical confidence.[9]

Sometimes God makes a decision about how to accomplish his purposes and chooses an individual to live out that extraordinary plan. It does not necessarily occur through an overwhelming experience with God, but through an opportunity that arises in someone's life that is part of a bigger story. That person has to make a choice to respond to the situation before them and participate in God's calling or turn away. David is one such example of supernatural selection in the Bible. In David we see God-confidence.

In the eyes of the world, young David was given clear, simple instructions:

> Take this sack of cracked wheat and these ten loaves of bread, and run them down to your brothers in the camp. And take these ten wedges of cheese to the captain of their division. Check in on your brothers to see whether they are getting along all right, and let me know how they're doing—Saul and your brothers, and all the Israelites in their war with the Philistines in the Oak Valley. (1 Samuel 17:17-19 *The Message*)

David was the baby of eight brothers, and he spent his days either playing the harp for Saul or tending sheep. Very ordinary. His father, Jesse, casually asked him to check in on the family, carry some food to them, and to report back. This was not a world-shaking assignment. And yet, God had greater plans—plans that included David. A fierce battle was being waged against the Israelites, and God wanted to demonstrate his authority. God chose David to accomplish the work of the Lord. To get it started, all David would do is ask a question.

"Who is this uncircumcised Philistine that he should defy the armies of the living God?" (1 Samuel 17:26) was a valid question from someone who loved God. Most of us will ask a similar question when someone we love is being mocked by a stranger. "Who does this guy think he is?" The thing is, this guy was no joke. Goliath stood about ten feet tall and carried around 126 pounds of armor. For forty days, he had been calling out to the Israelites, daring someone to come out and fight him. And the stakes were no laughing matter, either. Whoever won would have the losing nation as slaves. Days passed, and Goliath bellowed, and nothing happened. But this day, while David was carrying out his non-world-shaking assignment of delivering bread and cheese to his brothers, he heard the giant taunting the people of God. David responded, "Who does this guy think he is?"

The key for David was that he saw the Israelites not as the armies of Saul but as the armies of God. Saul and his army were terrified. But the army of God has no reason to fear. Big or not, Goliath was no match for God.

David was offended that no one stood up the God he served, loved and believed in with all his heart. While God caught

Moses's attention with the burning bush, David spontaneously—without prior motivation from God (at least as communicated in the Bible)—took on Goliath in defense of God's honor. God-confidence was instinctive on David's part.

We know that Moses, out of impulse, killed a man to defend the honor of an Israelite slave. David's act in killing Goliath was different, though. This was not impulsive, it was a calling—a God-ordained moment that unified the Israelites and restored honor to their God. Impulsive acts are usually carried out in our own strength, and while they may bring euphoria, that euphoria is usually fleeting. Such impulsive acts are missing the miraculous and point not to God but to our human nature. We become the victor as opposed to God winning the moment. The confidence in God and his pulling off the victory makes the difference.

When David volunteered to compete against Goliath, he was met with resistance. According to the king, such a contest required age, training, experience, proper weapons and a whole lot of armor. And when he looked at David, Saul saw none of those preparatory requirements. It seems odd that credentials were still important to Saul, given how many people holding these qualifications (including him) were out on the battlefield without taking up Goliath's challenge. Nevertheless, after David announces that there's no need to lose hope because he's ready to fight, the king quickly points out, "You can't go and fight this Philistine. You're too young and inexperienced—and he's been at this fighting business since before you were born." (1 Samuel 17:33 *The Message*). I can almost see Saul turning away to move onto other business after he says this. It's an open and shut case. No one on the battlefield had the courage to tell David the obvious truth that he was no match for Goliath, so it fell to King Saul, who laid it out with no room for argument. It's logical. It's clear. There's nothing else to talk about.

But David is not intimidated by Goliath, or King Saul for that matter. He responds in eloquent detail, sharing his personal testimonies of how the living God has brought him victory against beasts who've tried to attack his sheep. His stories demonstrate his courage and give all the credit to God. They demonstrate *kingdom imagination,* which has filled him with *God-confidence.*

David passionately impresses on Saul his confidence that God will hand him victory when he faces the Philistine, just as God has handed him victories against the beasts of the field. David does not invent credentials he doesn't have, making up lies to bolster his fighting resume. He doesn't try to argue with Saul's point and say, "Oh, those things— the armor, the advanced weaponry, the military training— mean nothing." Nor does David try to explain himself or beg the king for a chance. He can only offer his own experience, which is that God has continually given him victory against his foes. He expresses his faith in God to remain true to this record.

Now, I imagine this speech must have been pretty passionate to get the go-ahead from Saul. You'll remember that a lifetime of slavery is on the line for the people of God. It would be a step of faith not only for David, but for Saul and all the people of Israel. This call that David feels at the time is about defending God's honor, not about rescuing people like Moses did when he acted in killing the Egyptian soldier. David was chosen for this moment in time, and this battle was not for him but for the honor of God and the life of Israel whom God had chosen him to represent.

Of course, the king doesn't plan to throw all caution and logic to the wind. He immediately suits David up for the battle. David was nearly unable to move with all this stuff on him—armor he wasn't used to. He has to take it off. He removes the breastplate, the helmet and the sword before heading down to the brook with his staff, sling and shepherd's pack. There, he collects five smooth stones. How ridiculous David must have looked to the other soldiers! As if his age and inexperience weren't enough to make this entire errand seem foolish, the boy ditches all the proven gear in favor of some rocks. There he is, headed to fight a giant with a tunic and five stones. But David is determined to fight and he is confident that God is with him and has chosen him for this task.

Are we absolutely confident in God's victory? David's extraordinary life may feel out of reach, but in reality, he is a relatable young man God chose to use even when it didn't make sense.

I can't help but to think that, as Americans especially, self-confidence may not be our issue at all. I am reminded of the many contestants that look to make it "big" in entertainment by auditioning for *American Idol* and other reality competitions. We are entertained by the delusions that some people have, actually thinking that they sing well when in fact they sound horrific. William Hung was the first of a long line of people who have convinced themselves that they sound good. Could it be that we don't see more Davids today because we have adorned ourselves with self-confidence, to the point that we can barely move? Are we making up for a lack of the God-confidence David had that would allow us to do the extraordinary things God has in mind for us?

What is the difference between David and William Hung? Is there any difference in today's world? William perhaps was arrogant in his declaration that he was a great singer. David can't be described here as arrogant; his confidence was not in himself but in his God. David's perspective is better described as *audacious;* by the standards of the day he was a runt—he could not even fit into the armor offered him—but nevertheless he believed not that he could defeat a giant but that God would deliver him as he had in the past, would deliver Israel as he had in the past. David was bold and courageous based on past experiences; William was delusional and egotistical in his declaration of his own brilliance. David stands in the midst of a challenging situation and declares that God will deliver.

Where is God-confidence today? David was a young man with an ordinary life; he played harp for the king, tended his father's sheep, carried food to his family, stood up to a giant and by God's grace delivered his people from a return to slavery. What if God has selected you to fight for his people?

You may feel that you are underqualified for such an extraordinary assignment. You may have average school grades or simply lack educational credentials. Maybe your job is not one that society respects or honors, and you find that others disregard you and your efforts. Perhaps your background is unimportant. You are a regular person from an unknown place. You know that feeling of being seen as insignificant. The world may see your story as small, but you can be certain that God is present in it and that he is calling you to something that will require a kingdom imagination and God-confidence on your part. You may be chosen by God, like David. God may be calling you to face the giants of this world. Your everyday challenges are all you need to be prepared and confident as God chooses to use you mightily.

5

Spirit-Led Mentors

ESTHER AND PETER'S STORIES

Self-confidence, as we have said, can be developed by human means. It begins when we are small children and our parents or caretakers celebrate our smallest accomplishments. They clap when we take a step, learn to ride a bike or participate in a spelling bee. The daily successes are highly celebrated. This encouragement builds our confidence to try that next new step, sport, presentation or endeavor. Most of us have had a champion support us at some point, at some level, in our lives. Unfortunately the opposite is also true: when there is an absence of positive reinforcement in our lives, it can lead to major insecurities. In fact, neglect and abuse can bring about catastrophe, resulting in poor behavior, anxiety or depression.

Very early on, we learn to intuitively respond to positive reinforcement and encouragement. Later in life, the opposite begins to happen. Voices connect with the deep insecurities of our hearts and remind us (or tell us) what we cannot do.

Naysayers speak to every new step, predicting you'll lose or be embarrassed or fail. They expound on the risk and encourage you to remain in safe spaces. These voices can be loud and painfully consistent. They cause us to hesitate and plead with our soul to lay low.

The way to break free of such paralyzing negativity is to have people in your life who will not let you live beneath your potential—wonderful people who continue drawing us out to live in God's best for our lives. They see something in us before we are able to see it. Even if they don't know exactly where God is calling us, they push us to seek it out and discover his greater purpose. They remind us how great we can be and confirm that we have much to offer to others. They speak positively of our endeavors. And when we start to throw ourselves a pity party, these individuals won't allow too much wallowing and instead minister to us through affirmation and encouragement. They spark something in us that brings our soul to life.

These agitators push us to places where we would never have gone if it had not been for their constant prodding. They are special people because, unlike parents with trusting children, they are often working with people who have failed, been damaged, are fearful or are simply clueless.

There are people today who are experiencing their transformation from ordinary to extraordinary through the loving encouragement of Spirit-led mentors. Esther is one such person, and Mordecai, her uncle, was one such mentor. The only thing not ordinary about Esther was her indescribable beauty. Her appearance attracted attention and earned her favor. However, God had extraordinary plans for her life that would outshine any physical beauty she may have possessed. She had kingdom purposes, but it took Mordecai to encourage her and push her forward into that extraordinary life.

Esther, in fact, may never have stepped into her extraordinary purposes if it were not for Mordecai. He heard of the king's decision to search for a new wife, and he thought about Esther. She, on the other hand, seemed clueless as to her qualifications for this honor and did not foresee her role as queen. When Mordecai encouraged her to pursue it, I imagine that laughter, doubt and fear filled her mind and heart. Nevertheless, Mordecai continued to remind Esther that she is beautiful.

I wonder if this was the first time that Mordecai ever affirmed Esther. It must have been devastating for Esther to lose her parents and wind up living with her uncle, and now here he was caring for her into adulthood. Perhaps he often shared with her his love and adoration, but now he was telling her that she could be queen. A young woman who loses her parents (and maybe some of her confidence in the aftermath) is now being encouraged to be queen.

I realize that using the word *encouraged* here might be a bit of a stretch, given the cultural implications of the time in regards to woman. Esther could have felt as though she was being commanded to go and see if she could be queen, but even given that as a possibility the dialogue between her and Mordecai suggests admiration of Esther and an expectation of divine influence—and, yes, hope for the best for Esther.

Special encouragers like Mordecai believe for us when we

do not see ourselves. They often see our potential, who we will become, and believe it more than we do ourselves. When I was in high school, I decided that any good thing that happened in my life was probably an accident and would eventually turn into something bad. A youth leader at my church, however, wouldn't let me get away that easily. He would not let me give into the fear that gripped my heart. Every week, he would affirm and encourage the deepest parts of my heart and confidence. *You are something special! That was great insight! Man, you are good at this!* Week after week, he sowed these seeds in my heart, and soon I began to run to his class and looked forward to spending as much time with him as possible. I could feel the difference he was inspiring in me. That's what I think was going on between Esther and Mordecai. Mordecai believed for Esther. I imagine she entered the search for a queen as much to please Mordecai as to actually seek after the position.

As you may know or have already guessed, Esther did become queen, and it wasn't long before she lost touch with what was going on outside the palace—until one day, when a servant came to her and told her that her uncle was mourning over the looming decimation of the Israelites at the hands of Haman, special advisor to the king. Esther sent Mordecai food and clothes, but he refused them, reminding Esther that such extraordinary times did not call for an ordinary queen. She had been chosen to be queen, but for an extraordinary task. Mordecai encouraged Esther to stand up and enter into God's purpose for her placement in the palace. *For such a time as this*, he told her.

Led by the Spirit, Mordecai pushed Esther toward the place where she could say, "If I perish, then I perish." Inspired by Mordecai's challenge, Esther set aside the comforts of her position and decided to take on the responsibility of approaching the king. Some of the people in our lives are put there to ensure our path to the extraordinary life and then hold us accountable to the call. Has someone been pushing you to set aside your comfort and realize God's call on your life? Give thanks for this person! Open yourself to listen to God-led voices that encourage you and spur you on to seek out and fulfill his extraordinary purposes.

SATURATED BY GRACE

Imagine you are at your job on a regular Tuesday. You are working hard. It's been a long day, one where you were not able to meet most of your goals. You feel discouraged and tired. Near the end of your shift, as you are preparing to go home, you notice that your coworkers are gathering. Though this is unusual, you are tired and don't care to pay much attention. But then you notice the man that the group is surrounding begins to walk straight toward you. You have heard of him because he helped your mother-in-law in some way. He inquires about your work and asks you to put in a couple more hours. You sigh, but oblige because you know it will please your spouse. You do, however, not so subtly mention that you are tired and have worked all night with no success. "Still," you say. "I'll try again since you asked."

In the next few moments you are shocked as you discover that you and your coworkers are having the most success of the entire day. Instantly, you recognize a miracle was just performed. You look at the man. This act confirms everything you had been hearing. Wait—wasn't it actually that this man had *healed* your mother-in-law? This moment changes your life in an instant. You believe the man is sent from God, so you quickly declare to him, "I am a sinner." *I am not worthy. Do not expect much.*

The man smiles and invites you to follow him. You accept, leaving everything you know to follow. You are changed by the abundant grace that is offered. Your life is no longer ordinary. You have crossed in the realm of the extraordinary.

From the moment he left everything to follow Christ, Peter's life was a roller coaster ride—right up to Jesus' crucifixion. Peter would proudly announce, "You're the Christ, the Messiah, the Son of the living God." Jesus came back:

> God bless you, Simon, son of Jonah! You didn't get that answer out of books or from teachers. My Father in heaven, God himself, let you in on this secret of who I really am. And now I'm going to tell you who you are, really are. You are Peter, a rock. This is the rock on which I will put together my church, a church so expansive with energy that not even the gates of hell will be able to keep it out. (Matthew 16:16-18 *The Message*)

But there were other times where Jesus would be forced to rebuke Peter for his lack of understanding and wisdom. And, of course, Peter is infamous for his three denials as Jesus is being led to his trial and execution. Peter is called out as a Christ-follower three times, and he lies all three times because he is afraid and starts to doubt. The same person who readily declared that Jesus was the Christ later abandons him whole-heartedly. What a low moment for Peter.

After Jesus is raised from the dead, he begins to appear to the disciples. Having retreated to their old lives, having gone back to what was familiar, they had returned themselves to an ordinary life. Jesus had to repeat the initial invitation when he called them from the boat three year earlier. Peter finds himself face to face with Jesus again in a dialogue that pours grace down on Peter's life. *Peter, do you love me? Peter, do you love me? Peter, do you love me?*

Affirming his love for Jesus three times, Peter is restored, and Jesus acknowledges the bountiful forgiveness. This experience with grace changes Peter completely and forever.

For some, the transition from ordinary to extraordinary comes through a moment where God's inexplicable grace transforms. Maybe you've gone back to your old ways in hopes of gaining freedom or control. Or maybe you have made mistakes that feel epic, and they have caused doubt to increase and have pushed you to keep walking further and further away from what you know God has called you to. Can you relate to Pete's doubt, fear, and confusion? Have you held tightly to control of your own life?

When Donna and I first discerned a call to serve God as urban missionaries, there was an initial sense of joy. We felt energized by what we were doing, even during trials. We felt at the center of God's calling on our lives. But then we entered a painfully "lean" season. There were times we would have no idea where the next meal was coming from. There were times our children needed clothing. Times without healthcare. We had years of no steady pay. We would imagine dreams of how to do our work better, but we had no resources to accomplish our dreams. Doubt grew in me.

So I went back to my ordinary life. I took a part-time job to relieve some of the stress. I loved the work, and I quickly gained the respect of my supervisors and peers. I received encouragement in my work, requested a promotion and finally had steady pay. This work made me feel I had an answer to those who criticized the wisdom of my decision to become a missionary in the first place.

These benefits were all good, but God wanted something different for me. This job was my expression of grasping for control, of taking the role of providing for my family away from God. I tried to reason with God. It didn't make sense to give up health benefits with three children. I only had to work four hours each morning, so the rest of my day was committed to ministry. Besides, now the ministry didn't have the burden of paying me much. In addition, I was a positive influence of the gospel among those I worked alongside each day. It all sounded good, but I was not doing what God wanted me. My call to be a missionary and to trust God was clear. I needed God to forgive me for wandering away and stealing back control. He extended grace, and an extraordinary life grew.

God wants to shower you in his grace, and that grace will sustain you as you enter an extraordinary life. Peter's extraordinary life took off after Pentecost, when the Holy Spirit descended on a room full of Christ-followers. Peter was right there, and the world soon began to change as Peter preached the gospel with power.

The "ordinary" person is led to extraordinary experiences when they are explicitly commissioned by God (like Moses); or they are thrust by circumstance into a timely mission (like Esther); or they are confronted head-on with evil and outright defiance of a divinely-ordered world (like David); or they are confronted in their weakness, folly and sin by the God who created them and who nevertheless desires to befriend them (like Peter). All ordinary people, all met with extraordinary experiences, all watched over by an extraordinary God. We are like them; we can all move toward a place in God where we begin living above our circumstances and bring honor to the God we love and serve.

6

Job Versus Calling

"Everybody can be great . . . because anybody can serve. You don't have to have a college degree to serve. You don't have to make your subject and verb agree to serve. You only need a heart full of grace. A soul generated by love."

MARTIN LUTHER KING JR.

There is great emphasis in our society on working, and rightfully so. We work to feed our families, pay for shelter, and care for ourselves. When choosing a place of employment, one of the major considerations we evaluate is the pay. This number determines our standard of living. It is possible, however, that many of us have overemphasized the monetary benefit of working, and therefore, have turned people away from their calling from God to search instead for work based primarily on the pay scale.

This type of employment I call a job.

A job is simply the task we do to get paid. Inherently, there is nothing wrong with a job, but I do worry that an underlying message focused on monetary gain as the major goal may be a recipe for disaster in the long run. We go to jobs, perform tasks and receive a benefit. We can execute jobs without being deeply connected. We are able to arrive at the start of our day, work very hard and expel emotional energy. We might even work extra hours if it means extra pay. Typically, it's not a problem to separate a job from one's "real life." Whether employed as a housekeeper, social worker, banker, chaplain, police officer or cook, all these jobs are important. However, most people wouldn't hesitate to walk away from a job once the check went away.

Calling is different. Calling inspires a deeper commitment to your work. Calling pushes a person to ask significant questions about what they do with their lives—questions such as *Who am I? What are my gifts and talents? How is my life being shaped by this work? What life would remaining in this work make impossible for me?* Calling pushes us deeper into ourselves when choosing a college, or taking an internship. It doesn't allow us to jump at every opportunity simply because it pays more. We take personal responsibility about our life direction and choices.

We must step outside the one criterion of pay and explore all the different aspects of our work and how they connect to the calling Christ has placed in our heart.

Sometimes, our calling will defy reason and require us to leave jobs of safety and success. Rodger and Tina were enjoying a wonderful life together. He worked as an engineer after graduating near the top of his class. She had obtained her master's degree and was a teacher at a local elementary school. They had been married six years, had two beautiful children and lived in a wonderful home on the northeast side of Philadelphia in Germantown. They were committed followers of Jesus and were raising their children in a Christian home, including weekly Bible study, church involvement and a home devotional life.

From the outside, nothing seemed problematic about their life together. Still, neither Rodger nor Tina could shake the unsettled feeling in their souls. They both fostered an ache to do something more with their lives. They nurtured dreams of teaching and training children, using the Bible as their basis. They found themselves faced with a crazy dilemma. Should they continue working at their two jobs that paid very well, even if it wasn't where they felt called? Or should they become faith missionaries with an organization that teaches the Bible to children around the world? On the one hand, they could continue enjoying the luxuries that had become accustomed to having, driving the car they wanted, and living in a home and neighborhood of their choosing. The other decision would require them to give up secure work for a pure faith endeavor.

They could not shake the call. The jobs they were in, though important, felt empty compared to the work God had laid on their hearts. Rodger and Tina could not ignore God's calling on their lives and chose to follow it. In response, an African American engineer and a teacher, with their two small children, decided to raise financial support and become missionaries in their own city. This is extraordinary.

Donna and I met this extraordinary couple in 1990, just

after we had just made the same decision for ourselves. Rodger and Tina had been living in the city for over fifteen years when God crossed our paths with their family; their children were in college, and years of God supplying their every need was already a part of their story. They confidently advised us that if God were calling us, he would supply the resources. Their decision was not a logical one, but they explained that is was based solely on God's desires. He had a plan to be carried out, and he had asked Rodger and Tina to participate in his agenda. They could not say no.

Sometimes our career choice falls right in line with the calling God has placed on our hearts. Our friend Janice, for example, had a gift helping people and enjoyed making them feel comfortable all of her life. As a young girl, when family would come to stay over, she would be sure everyone had a pillow for the night. She took cold drinks to her dad when he would work around the house. It truly brought her joy to comfort others.

When Janice was in high school, she was offered the opportunity to study abroad one summer or to be a candy striper at the local hospital. She decided to fill the candy striper position. It was the best summer of her life as she guided patients through the hospital and shared smiles with those who were nervous or in pain. She took small gifts to the patients and held the hand of a scared mother waiting for her child to come through an operation.

After that summer, there was no doubt in Janice's mind what she would study in college. It seemed God had been preparing her to be a nurse her entire life. And so she did go on to nursing school, and shortly after graduation she was offered a job at the same hospital from her high school days. Janice served faithfully, and she was soon promoted to the head nursing position on her floor. The area she oversaw was, by far, the most respected floor in the hospital. The nurses she supervised adored her, and it was a daily scene to see patients in tears, hugging Janice upon being discharged. Janice was truly extraordinary.

Janice is also a follower of Jesus. She attends church each week, sings in the choir, and does health screening awareness days at her church. Janice was called (she might even say created) to be a nurse, and she sees each day as an offering of her life to the God she loves. Janice does not just work in nursing, although she gets a pay check, but she has given her life in service. She would acknowledge that she has been caring for people from as early as she can remember. She has taken what might seem ordinary—offering a pillow, sharing a cold drink—and offered it to God who multiplied her offering to do extraordinary things.

Sometimes we are aware that our job is not really God's calling on our life. Still, we don't sense that God has instructed us to leave it behind for a new endeavor. Sometimes, our calling may run parallel to the work we call a job. One example is my friend Rob. Rob absolutely hated his job. It was not what he had planned on doing. He had run out of money before he could finish college, but he didn't want to take out more loans. He was in college one semester, and then he was dumping out trash from offices in the middle of the night.

Rob's plan was to finish college slowly, taking one course at a time as he could pay for it and also clearing up his student loan debt. When we met, he was about halfway to earning his degree. Rob was a very smart man who always had a book in his hand. He would give great insight if you had the patience and determination to get it out of him. Still, even in his best moments, there was absolutely no denying that he did not like his job or most of the people around him. He was often a bitter person. His 6-feet, 3-inch stature, deep voice and intense stare intimidated most people, giving the impression he was going to annihilate you at any moment.

Rob intrigued me, so I made efforts to get to know him. He highly respected hard work, and since I was a diligent worker, he would talk with me, especially when we worked together on projects during the midnight shift. I soon learned that Rob was a Christian, but he didn't care much for church. He attended a couple times a month and gave money to things he thought were worthwhile. Rob and I spent many working nights discussing life, marriage, hopes and dreams.

I discovered that Rob had a soft spot in his heart for young men with potential but no resources to realize it. Their situations resonated with him because it was also his story. What I figured out about Rob was that while he hated his job and made no bones about it, what he mainly despised was how people were treated on the job. He cringed at the way supervisors talked to employees. He disliked the way the schedule was organized. He didn't appreciate that if you were five minutes late getting back from break, someone would talk to you like a child and write you up, regardless of the job you had done well. And, most important, he hated the way people cleaning offices were looked down on. I learned that Rob cared more about the people working than most others.

A supervisor's position opened up one day, and as was the custom, it was posted for the staff and employees first, so they could apply for it if they chose to do so. This had happened many times before, but this particular night, Rob asked me if I thought he should put in for it. He asked me if I thought he would do a good job. I affirmed both. Rob applied for the job and because he had been there so long, he was granted an interview. He was given the position, and Rob worked hard from that point on to improve the workplace.

When I asked Rob why he decided to go after the promotion this time, he told me it was because he felt he had something to offer. He wanted to change the work environment. I could only imagine at this point what Rob may have been wrestling with. Maybe he was even at a crossroads—a decision he had to make about himself and why he was in this job. Had his kingdom imagination kicked in so that he now saw something beyond what was right in front of him and embraced this as an opportunity? Did he just get tired of emptying trash? I am not sure what caused this shift in Rob but something was causing a shift. He was now imagining life differently—a redemption of his thoughts, if you will, from the narrow to the big, from the self to others.

Rob took his ordinary life of cleaning offices and emptying trash cans, a life which felt like a failure to him, and he made an offering of it. He didn't leave his employment, nor did he realize God had placed these tasks in his heart as a calling. Rather, he discovered the ways God was calling him to serve and care for his coworkers through leadership. His simple job transformed into a calling to help people, and Rob's life became extraordinary. Rob's transformation also created an environment where others could experience grace and perhaps see their contribution as important. Extraordinary calling lifts, inspires and creates on roads for grace to be established and experienced.

When we stop to think about it, we want those around us working for more than simply their paycheck. What type of care can you really receive from the doctor who is just doing his job? And what about a pastor who only preaches to cash his paycheck? Sometimes it even feels difficult ordering a hamburger from someone who is clearly there just to clock in and clock out. In all the areas of our lives, we are blessed and encouraged by those who are working out the calling God has placed on their lives. We hope that those taking care of our children, our health, educating us, or ministering to us love what they are doing and truly have a deeper understanding and commitment to their work.

Life-giving work is available to all of us. But we must alter our primary question from "How much money can I make?" Instead, we must explore those areas where we can serve. How can I take what I am doing, what I believe I was made to do, or what I feel God may be calling me to do, and turn it over to God? In this offering, we can count on him to transform our offering into something extraordinary. We must let God use our lives to change the world, draw people to him, and offer hope in desperate situations. That calling bring excitement, engagement and much more motivation than money can provide.

7

Risking Safety

This resurrection life you received from God is not a timid, grave-tending life. It's adventurously expectant, greeting God with a childlike "What's next, Papa?" God's Spirit touches our spirits and confirms who we really are. We know who he is, and we know who we are: Father and children.

ROMANS 8:15-16 *The Message*

My family and I had the opportunity to go on a mission trip to Mexico City some years ago. We were visiting a couple serving there, and they took us to visit many villages outside of the city. One of these communities had no electricity. Their water supply was contained in barrels, filled daily by what seemed to be the local water company. The roads there were so incredibly dusty that when someone drove by, you would crouch to avoid the thick cloud that would form. Many children developed diarrhea due to the intense dust. It was here that we met Mary, a 4-foot, 9-inch tall blonde woman. She had set up a clinic to care for pregnant women and their children. Mary was a missionary with a Catholic diocese in the United States, and she had moved to Mexico specifically to help the people of this village. She talked excitedly of her work in the village and all she was learning from the people, whom she spoke of as if they were family. My heart was moved as she described her work.

Because I asked, Mary informed me that she is not supported in her mission. The church from which she came had sent support for a while but then stopped, asking her to return home. She complied, but then felt compelled to return. In her explanation, she spoke as though she had been created to exist right here in this community, despite the health risk, despite poor water quality, despite the deeply dark nights and the dusty days. She relocated to another country without support or finances to develop a clinic that was caring for countless mothers who would otherwise go without care. This required incredible risk, but the kingdom of God was growing. This ordinary woman offered her entire life, accepted the risk, and placed herself in God's hands. The offering was received, the risk documented on the heart of Jesus, and the world changed.

Safety has become one of the major gods of our time. Everyone is familiar with the philosophy of "Safety First!" and we do everything we possibly can to keep safety the priority. It has even become one of the major drivers (if not sometimes the main one) in our decision-making processes. There is big business in selling the many products that promise us safety. A person now needs a home alarm system, car alarms, a cell phone and insurance on everything, all to "protect" ourselves.

The lengths we will go to in hopes of keeping safe can be amusing. A visiting friend of mine found a great deal for a rental car at $20 a day. But at the counter with the rental agent, he was talked into paying $15 a day extra for insurance and another $6 a day for the GPS device. Both were sold under the auspice that he would be a bit safer, especially driving through the dangerous city. The cost of the "safety features" was more than the cost of the car. So what was he doing? Was he renting a car or trying to purchase a "safe" visit to my city?

The internal message lurking behind the overt message of safety is fear. We have bred a society trapped in fear. And that insidious fear hinders us greatly.

Wikipedia is a "free encyclopedia that anyone can edit"; it has a respectable track record of accuracy, but more than that, it serves as something of a cultural consensus, a thermometer on culture, because it gives us the popular perspective of our society on various topics. Wikipedia features a lengthy definition of *safety*. Our friends and neighbors have put together the following explanation:

> Safety is the state of being "safe," the condition of being protected against physical, social, spiritual, financial, political, emotional, occupational, psychological, educational or other types or consequences of failure, damage, error, accidents, harm or any other event which could be considered non-desirable. Safety can also be defined to be the control of recognized hazards to achieve an acceptable level of risk. This can take the form of being protected from the event or

from exposure to something that causes health or economical losses. It can include protection of people or of possessions.

I can't help but wonder if our idea of safety actually separates us from people. When we think of places and people as "not safe," do we create walls that cause pain and misunderstanding? Do we keep ourselves away from certain people because we deem them unsafe? I am not talking about people who would bring harm such as in cases of robbery or abuse. I mean people who may be in places we would not dare go because they are in "unsafe" places—places that may not be protected from harm for whatever reason. I had a mom once come to drop of her daughter in Philadelphia to serve for a year there, but when the mom saw where her daughter's team would be living, she declared, "My daughter is not staying here. It is not safe." Thankfully her daughter did stay and went on to have a great year, but imagine how many people and (how much life-change) would have been missed if she would have acted on her mom's desire for her to be "safe."

This goal of safety drives many of our decisions, such as where we live, where our kids go to school, even where we will go to do something as insignificant as watching a movie. "Is it safe?" This question rings in our psyche over and over again. Of course, the reality is that what we mean by *being* safe is only what *feels* safe. While there are ways of minimizing our risk, there is nothing that can guarantee our protection and well-being. There are only gadgets and choices that make us think we are safe.

Meanwhile, when safety becomes a priority measure in

our lives, I believe it traps us in the ordinary. Our kingdom imagination is limited when we stop risking for the gospel. The question for me is this: Are we willing to knowingly take risks? Are we prepared to turn over our fears and insatiable need to feel safe to God as an offering? Are we willing, for the sake of the kingdom, to face dangers head on, knowing that we cannot even pretend to protect ourselves from the consequences?

A major aspect of the search for safety centers on control. The idea is that the more we can control a situation, the safer we can make it. We want to influence the outcomes as much as possible. The concept of entering a situation and not being in charge is, for some of us, a completely overwhelming thought. But in a theological sense, control is illusory. Does God give up his control to us? The answer is absolutely not. God asks us to trust him to protect us, but he does not give up or share control.

What then is risk? It is not wild, indiscriminate actions, but rather the ability to count the cost of an action. Risk in a theological sense is understanding the reality of a given situation—its capacity to cause us inconvenience or even harm—and then surrendering that given reality to the larger reality that our kingdom imagination and our God-confidence offer us. Our personal risk is then placed in the context of the greater good—God's dream for the world we find ourselves in. Any risk is (or ought to be) acceptable if it is in service to the greater good, and if we trust that the greater good will establish itself regardless of the circumstances, then risk becomes functionally irrelevant.

I am not in any way making light of the fact that there are some types of risk beyond our control. Hunger and poor education are good examples. These are types of "risks" that don't get glorified and should not be tolerated. The call to risk in the sense I am advocating here is actually confronted by these other, intolerable risks; when my neighbor is hungry or suffering, is the inconvenience serving my neighbor might cause me, or the possible harm that could come to me, a legitimate concern? In some cases the things we risk may even be what ultimately offers hope to a "at risk" situations in our world and beyond our control.

Risk eliminates the smoke and mirrors of safety by pushing us to evaluate the things we have accumulated to feel safe and to recognize their true value and place in our lives. Again, the people-edited Wikipedia definition of *risk* is as follows: "the potential that a chosen action or activity (including the choice of inaction) will lead to a loss (an undesirable outcome)." When we take a risk, there is the possibility that things can go wrong. There is the chance that what we set out to do could completely backfire. Bob Lupton, who is a friend and mentor of mine and lives and works in Atlanta, had the vision to take the old Atlanta stockade, an old prison which had been closed for decades, and turn it into transitional housing for working people who needed an extra hand up to get back on their feet. The stockade was an old concrete structure that would have been torn down if it was not for the fact that demolition of a building with six-foot concrete walls in some places was way too expensive, and so it sat. The structure was full of trash and debris of all kinds, with water leaking through the concrete floors from years of neglect. Bob and a colleague looked at this overwhelming chaos and decided (they might say they were led) to take a risk on redeeming this awful space. They put their reputations, time, money and their whole selves on the line. Twenty years later, the old Atlanta stockade was now called Glencastle: sixty apartments serving families in transition. Its gorgeous architecture, marble floors and southern style porch serve as a place of beauty to the community instead of blight. The old stockade that was once a place of pain and tragedy now represents hope and redemption, all because a few instead of running from risk embraced it with vision and creativity.

The type of risk tolerance practiced by Bob and his colleague, if you will, works contrary to the risk aversion we so often see in society. The courage to go against the cultural norms is one that brings life and hope.

In a strange sort of way there is a danger whether we decide to take a risk or not. Simply not acting, while avoiding a short-term risk, may allow circumstances to worsen and become an even bigger problem. When we choose to do nothing, people can be hurt and evil continues. The Bible tells story after story of risk-takers, people who trusted that God's greater good was worth putting themselves on the line. Moses is instructed to approach Pharaoh without knowing God's plan for delivering the Israelites. Esther is compelled to speak on behalf of the Israelites without explicit permission to approach the king. Joshua and Caleb buck the majority opinion and advise Israel to take the land inhabited by giants. Gideon accepts the challenge from God to fight a war with only three hundred men. Daniel is convicted to bypass the king's meat and to eat differently than what society promoted as the "right way." Abraham obeys God by heading toward an altar to sacrifice his only son. When the apostle Paul writes the Philippian church from a jail cell, he notes that his audience for the gospel is limited there, and that meanwhile opportunists are taking advantage of his imprisonment to make a name for themselves. And yet he concludes that

> everything happening to me in this jail only serves to make Christ more accurately known, regardless of whether I live or die. They didn't shut me up; they gave me a pulpit! Alive, I'm Christ's messenger; dead, I'm his bounty. Life versus even more life! I can't lose. (Philippians 1:20-21 *The Message*)

These examples are among the hundreds we witness in Scripture where God requires risk from his followers, where he asks his servants to trust his direction, even though they don't know the outcome. Safety and control become nonissues when our eyes are opened to God's call on our lives.

Although we have the privilege to see God work when we trust him completely and without condition, this is not without cost. There is often a price to pay. The price may be the loss of friends or a change in how you relate to people close to you, which can be quite challenging. The cost is sometimes monetary, or we could have to give up some comforts that we enjoy. The asking price is not cheap. As Dietrich Bonhoeffer put it,

The disciple is dragged out of his relative security into a life of absolute security (that is, in truth, into the absolute security and safety and fellowship of Jesus), from a life which is observable and calculable (it is, in fact, quite incalculable), into a life where everything is unobservable and fortuitous (that is, into one which is necessary and calculable), out of the realm of finite (which is in truth the infinite) into the realm of infinite possibilities (which is the one liberating reality).[10]

What is "seen" and felt, of course, may not be as safe as we might like. But Scripture testifies to accounts where God asks a small thing of his followers, and it leads to large victory for them and the whole community. We are led to give up a certain amount of safety, and in doing so we find ourselves in the safest place possible—in step with God's kingdom plan.

Are there places in your everyday life where God is calling you to take a risk for the kingdom? Maybe you see someone being mistreated—a classmate being bullied, a friend disrespecting their spouse, an employer cheating the workers—and instead of remaining silent, you feel called to stand up and step in. Maybe you are clinging on to someone or something—a boyfriend or girlfriend, a job, a savings account—that you know God has asked you to relinquish. Maybe you know in your heart God is leading you to leave your current, comfortable life, but you are scared. The list of small risks we must take is endless. What we need to realize, though, is that in these risks, God's power is unleashed.

We're not really risking, I suppose, if we're throwing in

our lot with God; rather we're relinquishing the cultural mores and expectations that have declared certain things risky. We are valuing faith over security. We are really relinquishing our power over to God. We are letting him manage the details, trusting him to work things out.

Handing over the reigns of our lives is what God requires. Risk carries with it a deep sense of trust.

Trust in the LORD with all your heart
  and lean not on your own understanding;
in all your ways submit to him,
  and he will make your paths straight. (Proverbs 3:5-6)

I learned this verse first in Sunday school. The teacher at that time would pass out treats to all those who took the time to learn the assigned memory verse. My mother would insist that I learn it, and each evening I had to go over the verse in front of her. Come Sunday I was proud to stand up in class and show that I had it memorized (and collect my candy for the trouble). After becoming a preacher in my church, I chose this verse to expound on as one of my early sermons. It seemed like a simple enough message, one in which there was truth and a pattern to trusting God that would end in reward. Trusting and acknowledging God would lead to him directing our paths.

It was a good sermon, but it wasn't until years later that I felt the whole truth of it. In the summer of 2010 Mission Year hit a rough patch in our funding, one that challenged the board, staff and myself in our trust of God. We were deciding literally whether it was time to shut our doors. God came through, though, and ultimately we concluded that our understanding of the circumstances were getting in the way of our kingdom imagination: the need for Mission Year hadn't gone away, and our sense of call was still there. So we did our best to surrender our risk-aversion to God, and he came through. We not only ended that year but decided to start a new one as well.

The next summer we were not in as dire a position, but we did have needs to finish the year well, and we found that trusting God with the second year was more challenging than trusting him with the first. Relinquishing our lives to God means trusting him over and over again, and perhaps perpetual trust is much harder than mustering it up for a one time shot. We are instructed to trust as a continuous motion, perhaps relinquishing is this continuous process. I think the tendency is to trust when we really need it and then lean on ourselves the rest of the time. We should never lean on our own understanding, though, because when we do we make an effort to take the control back, to snatch the reins from God. When we relinquish our false sense of control, our obedient risk opens the door for him to enter our circumstances. We are not responsible for the end result, the change or lack thereof, but we are required to open our lives to God's leading, whatever the request. A sliver of space is all God needs to accomplish the miraculous. It is in these openings where we see change realized. That's the power of the extraordinary. Give God space over and over again. Take a risk, large or small, and watch God's presence active in and around us.

RELUCTANT DISCIPLES

My friend Carson sometimes describes his family as "reluctant disciples." By that he means the things that they enjoy and find comfortable, the things that give them a sense of security, sometimes get in the way of their capacity to trust God and pursue his calling on their lives. Here's Carson's story.

> A few years ago, we were living the life that many people hope to live: country club membership, status, recognition, influence, new cars, successful kids in private schools, nice home, private pool, three day weekends every week, travel, etc. And church, well, the American dream has become the standard for the American church as well. Because we had success in the world, we were given positions in the church. It is true that people associate Christian depth with success and/or charisma. But there was a holy discontent that was creeping into our hearts. We couldn't define it, but we knew it was present. Rather than embracing this discontent and seeking its source, we would mask the feelings with a new trip, new toy, or new experience. That is until . . .
>
> Receiving a phone call from our oldest son, our pacesetter, the appointed leader and example for our other sons, telling us that he is planning to interrupt his college education to live with the poor, challenged everything we valued. We were not unsupportive. Quite the opposite, we researched several organizations that presented such opportunities, and attempted to be a sounding board as he sought God's guidance in the decision

process. Our unstated thoughts, unstated to hide our shallowness, swirled as we considered the financial repercussions of such a decision. What if he chooses not to complete his college degree? He had such potential to succeed, prosper, lead, and live this American dream that we had bought into. And selfishly, we began to wonder, *How much more will we have to pay, and for how many years?* But we did want to support his heart and calling, so we made the arrangements and drove him to Chicago to participate in Mission Year. . . . We dropped him off in a neighborhood that looked nothing like the nice suburban neighborhood he had grown up in. Thus began a year that would change us all forever.

God took this opportunity to rekindle that holy discontent he had placed in our hearts. We began to realize that the American Dream may not be a Christian ideal. We began to ask ourselves the hard questions: Who are we? What have we become? How have we led our family? What will we one day leave behind? Are our lives making an impact? Is the world different because we have been here? We did not like the answers. So we began to seek the heart of our Father. He was so kind, accepting, and patient. We have learned that our Father is never anxious or in a hurry. He patiently waits for us to find him, and he gladly reveals himself to the degree that we seek him. He opened our eyes to the people around us—not our peers but the hurting, real world outside our isolated bubble—and we began to see people for who they are rather than what they could do for us.

Joe and Kelli tell a similar story of risk, misplaced security and the kind of life change God can generate when we give our ordinary lives to him.

(Joe) My wife, Kelli, has always had a heart of mercy and compassion. She has always challenged me to see others from God's perspective. We discussed how God was using our son, Clay, and how he was awakening my heart. I was not alone. Kelli had also been sensing that God had something more for us. So we sought his will with vigor and passion. Our church was participating in a twenty-one-day "Daniel fast," so we took this time to dive into God's Word and seek his heart. We each desired his voice to be the voice we heard, so as not to be influenced by one another, we chose not to discuss what we were hearing and sensing until after we had completed the fast. To our delight we had both clearly heard from God. To our disappointment, neither of us heard a clearly defined direction as to how his Word was to be accomplished. We felt like Abraham: God told him to go, and then he would show him where. We knew it was time to go, to change our priorities, to alter our course, but how?

(Kelli) A few weeks into Clay's Mission Year commitment, he spent a weekend in something called "PROP (Pauper's Right of Passage)." Basically, Clay and his teammates spent a couple of days living as "homeless" in the streets of Chicago. After this weekend experience, he phoned me and shared how most people that he encountered simply ignored him, pretending he was invisible. He shared how one woman even yelled at him. She told him how disgusting he was and that he should go get a job "like the rest of us." As I listened to him, my first feeling was one of outrage. "How dare they treat *my* son that way?" But, as I continued to listen to his description of the weekend, and how it had impacted his life, I began to feel a deep conviction from God. I soon realized that my son had encountered me on the streets of Chicago that weekend. No, I wasn't physically present, but how many times had I passed by a homeless person and refused to look them in the eye? How many times had I crossed to the other side of the street so that I could avoid an encounter with someone I considered "beneath" me? How sad this made me. In fact, I hung up the phone and wept. Over the next several days and weeks, I realized that I did not want life to go on as usual. I began to realize that it was time to make a change—a radical change—in life as we knew it. It was time to walk the walk, and stop only talking the talk.

The word we both kept hearing was the word *unencumbered*. We knew we were bound to something that was preventing our movement into his heart. So we began looking at our lifestyle, and what we discovered is what many of us find when we slow down enough to look and listen. It's funny (or sad) that no matter how much you make, you want more. We had lived in a pattern of excess, and we were bound by debt: car notes, mortgage, credit cards, and a business that demanded stability and did not allow much flexibility. How could

we move at the impulse of God if we were bound, en-
cumbered . . .

And there was the answer. We realized that our greatest asset and greatest shackle was our family dental
practice. We began an exploration into the possibility of
selling our dental practice. That would be no small feat.
God had blessed us tremendously and the practice had
grown quite successful. We were ranked in the top 2
percent of dental practices in the United States. That's
great, right? Well not in the fall of 2008. If you remember, the banking industry was on the brink of collapse
because of the huge mortgage crisis that had hit our nation. . . . We were told that a dental practice the size of
ours would take, on average, two years to sell, and that
it would take much longer because of the financial crisis inhibiting banks risking a small business loan. But,
what else were we to do? We felt confident that we were
doing the right thing, and if not, God would show us.
We have learned through years that it is much easier to
move at God's direction when you are already in motion. So in January 2009 we placed the practice on the
market with the expectation that we had two to three
years to prepare for our future. By then our oldest two
sons would be out of college, we could get out of debt
and be ready to move into whatever it was that God had
for us (no, we still had no idea what we were supposed
to do).

(Joe) Have you noticed that God's timing is not always your timing? Three weeks later we received a call

from our broker that we had a buyer for the dental practice, and a few months later we were unencumbered. So now what?

We waited, wondered, and like Abraham waiting to have a son that was promised, we began to take the future into our own hands. Joe began making phone calls, exploring job opportunities, putting together a résumé. We shared our journey with a pastor friend and were asked to share it again with our lead pastors. It was in their office that we began to discover our "Ur."

For many months our lead pastors had been praying that God would raise up a couple with a heart to serve the hurting of our city, and they believed that we were the answer to that prayer. Remember, Kelli is the one with the heart of mercy and compassion. I was more about leadership, potential and building something sustainable, not about spending time with people who apparently just did not have the drive to succeed. After all, if they just were more ambitious or worked harder, couldn't they have what I have? But it did seem that everyone else was hearing from God that this is the direction we should go, so I knew this must be the place to start.

We began the way every ministry should begin. We saw a need, looked at what we had in our hands and used it to meet the need. We took food and water to the homeless of our city. At the leadership of Kelli, we began a relationship with a homeless man. Through that relationship we began to see the trials and hurdles that are presented to those who have fallen to the bottom of the barrel. We learned that they are mostly men and women who have been dealt difficult hands, compounded by a bad decision or two, and lost hope. You see, when you lose hope, you give up. And when you give up, you give in to whatever is around you. For those living in the streets, what is around them is a trap from which there is little chance of escape.

We discovered that life is lonely on the streets. Because of the danger, there is distrust. Because of the distrust, there develops a protective instinct to isolate yourself from everyone else. Men or women who would share a meal with one another, a beer, or a variety of easily available drugs did not even know one another's names. They stand in single file lines, humiliated and defeated, to obtain proof of identification, food, clothing or a bed if they can find the money needed to gain access to the local mission.

On Saturdays we would spend time with the children of a local public housing development. So many children malnourished, unkempt, and un-nurtured. They live in homes without fathers, in the care of a young teenage mother who has been and continues to be abused and neglected herself. And the cycle continues. Welcome to life in urban/poor America; land of the free, and home of the brave. And many of us live in our country club world, attend our country club churches, and complain that we have to subsidize this lifestyle.

What a wake-up call for us. We live in Memphis, which was just recently identified as the "hungriest city in the United States." We have pastors who will not let that continue while we are God's ambassadors of peace and his active hands and feet in our city. So we have made it our task, our vision, our goal to make a difference and develop strategies to defeat the disease of poverty. Today we lead teams into the city of Memphis. We take food to and develop long term relationships with the homeless, helping them move forward into purpose and off of the street. We are actively developing housing and discipleship opportunities that include basic life skills, tackling addictions and negative identity mindsets. We are working with at-risk youth to provide encouragement and alternatives to gang activities. We are mentoring young mothers and helping prevent families from being separated because of poverty. We are launching a feeding program for the children of Memphis to provide nutritious meals that they do not have access to outside of government furnished meals at school. We are providing a high-end store for families to "purchase" clothes and food for their families at minimal or no charge to them. And we are constantly seeking new doors of opportunity and new partners because we know that we cannot do this alone, and we know the blessing those who come alongside of us will receive.

God has and continues to provide everything we need as we have taken this step of faith. We have no idea where this will lead, but we are enjoying the journey. It is not easy. We sometimes miss the golf, long weekends and the new cars, but we would not trade this for anything in the world. We have met new friends, shared life with those that have an amazing voice but no platform from which to be heard. We have learned lessons from the mouth of God spoken through the lips of a child. And we are learning to love—really love: to listen without an agenda, to hold on no matter how difficult and messy, to lift up no matter how heavy the load because God is our strength. We have reluctantly taken a leap into the unknown and yet become convinced that God will not only catch us, but place us far above and provide far greater joys and possessions than anything we have left behind. And it all began because our son decided to postpone college for the privilege of living among the poor. We owe Mission Year and our son a debt we can never repay. For without their passion, courage, and commitment, we would never have gained the unsurpassing knowledge of sharing in the sufferings of Christ, and coming to know the power of his resurrection (Philippians 3:10).

Clay, Joe and Kelli's son who participated in the Pauper's Rite of Passage, will finish this chapter with his story, from his Mission Year newsletter. It is intense and convicting, and it may at points rub you the wrong way. But it's a story of risk and of God's grace, and of an ordinary life being given over to the extraordinary.

[Living like paupers for us] began with us being taken to a homeless shelter where we were asked to fill out a form that was a requirement for anyone who stayed in the shelter. We were then taken to a room filled with do-nated clothes (mostly awkward sizes and obviously dis-carded clothing that people had no use for). We were told to pick out one shirt, one jacket, and one pair of pants (we were allowed to keep our socks and shoes). Those would be our clothes, and in fact our only items, for that night and the entire next day. After that we were provided a dinner consisting of a PB&J, soda, and a small bag of chips. They then took us to a small basket-ball gym, which had no heat and was quite dirty, and [we] were told goodnight. Needless to say, we weren't quite sure what to make of the sleeping situation. It was around 40 degrees that night, and our only option of sleep was on a freezing cold, dirty gym floor with no blankets, sleeping bags, or pillows, nothing except the clothes we had picked out. Well, as you can imagine, I didn't get much sleep that night. Saturday morning we were woken up roughly around 7:00 am (I say roughly because I didn't have a watch). We were given another PB&J and were then given our assignment for the day. We each picked a partner and were told to head down-town and proceed to live as the homeless do. We were challenged to beg for money to buy lunch, to meet other homeless people downtown and to hear their stories, and to ask advice on how to best beg for money. Let me tell you, many interesting experiences occurred during that day, one of which will most vividly remain in my mind. You see, I was sitting on the steps leading down to the subway train, asking people for money as they passed me by (most of whom ignored me, acted distracted, clutched their purses tightly, or pulled their children close to them); but one lady in particular I will never forget. As she was walking down the steps I asked if she would mind sparing 25 cents so that I could get lunch. She turned and faced me, and then proceeded to say . . . "What is wrong with you? Can't you get a job? Why won't you work for your money?" I responded by saying I was merely trying to get some lunch, seeing as I hadn't eaten all day and it was nearly 2:00 p.m. She then said, "Well haven't you ever had a job? Oh, I bet I know what happened. You probably got fired for doing drugs or something didn't you? That's all you are is some drug addict aren't you?" I responded by telling her that jobs were just hard to come by. She then said, "You're pathetic, just pathetic. (Then reaching into her wallet, she pulled out a dollar.) I can't believe I'm giving this to you, because I know all you're going to spend it on is drugs or cigarettes," and continued on her original path.

Now, I'm sure at this point you feel shocked, and I'm sure you may even feel sorry for me. My response to you if you are feeling that way is this: Please DO NOT DARE. Please don't you dare feel sorry for me, someone who merely endured that under a façade of being homeless for one short day. I hope you realize, as I do now, that this is what those who are homeless deal with on a daily basis. I hope you might have a small glimpse into the feeling of being dehumanized, of having your dignity stripped, of being forced to beg just to get by every day.

And yes, I said forced. I was enlightened to the fact that there are plenty of jobs available, but rarely will a business employ someone who has been homeless. Why would they? I mean if they're homeless they must have something wrong with them, right? They must be messed up in the head or somehow disabled, right? They must not have any type of work ethic, right? Yea, that's what I used to think too. That is, until I realized that the only people friendly to me the entire day on the street were those that were homeless. The only ones who validated me as a human being and as someone worth their time were the homeless friends I made. After the weekend was finished, I went back to my apartment, crawled in my bed, pulled my warm blanket over me, and couldn't sleep. I couldn't sleep knowing that Tommy, Jacob, Charlie and the other homeless men and women I met were sleeping on the ground, wondering when, if at all, their next meal would come. Wondering if anyone would take the time to merely smile at them, to let them know that they mattered. I haven't slept well since, but I have gone back. I went and hung out with Tommy this week, and I'll tell you this, I think Tommy may quickly become one of the best friends I'll have this year. I urge you not to consider me as some sort of saint, some sort of martyr for what I went through this weekend. Instead I leave you with this. "If you have any encouragement from being united with Christ, if any comfort from his love, if any fellowship with the Spirit, if any tenderness and compassion, then *make my joy complete by being like-minded, having the same love, being one in spirit and in purpose.* Do nothing out of selfish ambition or vain conceit, but in humility consider others better than yourselves" (Philippians 2:1-3).

8

Blending In Versus Standing Out

To live is to choose. But to choose well,
you must know who you are and what you stand for,
where you want to go and why you want to get there.

KOFI ANNAN, General Secretary of the United Nations,
2001 Nobel Peace Prize winner

Trends dominate our society. Many of us regularly find ourselves caught up in the craze of the day, whether it's the hottest fashion style or the latest technology. Imagine a rushing river and the thousands of water molecules that are swept into the natural flow. We flow right along with the river of our world.

It may be hard for most of us to admit, but blending in is comfortable. We focus on peer pressure in adolescents, but the reality is that remnants of society pressures of conformity continue far into adulthood. Doing what is expected, whether in life choices or in material purchases, assures us of some acceptance. "Go along with the crowd" is not always the external message, but it has translated to internal pressure that we put on ourselves to be "relevant" in society. Sometimes, we blend in by remaining quiet, by not drawing attention to ourselves. We hope not to create a scene. *Go along with it . . . conform . . . buy this . . . wear that . . . blend in . . .* This is the message of the day. Are you disturbed?

Blending in, staying quiet and going along with popular opinion has caused followers of Jesus to miss opportunities to see God work. As we pile into churches, there are people and places neglected because we are in the popular place to worship instead of the needed place. Our continual participation in the consumerist trends of society binds our money up into car payments, expensive cell phone plans, and credit card debt, and prevents us from using our money freely for kingdom work. In addition, these financial ties restrict us to jobs with certain hourly requirements and minimum pay standards that limit our freedom to participate in the activities where God may be calling us. Our fear of being rejected by society places boundaries on what we will and won't say, do or expect as a follower of Christ. Conformity steals our ability to think critically about issues or make rational decisions about what we truly need or what God is asking. Instead, everyone else's actions push us to follow blindly. It's significantly easier to stop posing questions and to just float down the river.

If we are called as followers of Christ to be salt and light in our world, that entails being actively engaged in the culture we live in every day. By saying that, however, I am not saying we should sacrifice the authenticity of our friendships and interpersonal interactions to serve some underlying goal.[11] And involving ourselves in the culture makes us vulnerable to that, because a blending/trending culture values relationships less than it values what is cool.

While there is no one definition of cool (what is considered cool depends a lot on context), the term itself is widely used, a generally accepted standard that others can be pressured into pursuing. In a technology-obsessed society, the person without a cell phone or who still writes letters would be seen as foolish or antiquated. There are cool clothes, styles and principles, and along with these are people and products that embody them. Apple is cool. Prius is cool. Living downtown is cool. Twitter is cool. Wii is cool. President Obama is cool. Between the time I write this book and you read it these things may or may not still be cool. The culture of cool is not stable; you can have cool stuff one day—you can be the coolest person in the room—and tomorrow it could all vanish.

The culture of the kingdom, by contrast, counts on some solid truths that have stood the test of time: things like love, justice, service, friendship and peace. These are the things Jesus majored in when he walked the earth, and they are persistent and consistent over time. Trends come and go, but God's ways last forever, and the difference between an ordinary life and an extraordinary life is often the difference between pursuing the culture of the kingdom and indulging the culture of cool.

As we aspire to the extraordinary life God has for us, we should probably check our motives every now and then: are we simply following trends, or is our behavior being driven by our kingdom imagination and our God-confidence? Do we spend more time building the culture of cool than we do the culture of the kingdom? I recently read a startling account of a pastor who was brought up on charges for having sex with teenage boys. The account I read included quotes from people on the church staff who suspected this was happening, and one person even admitted witnessing the pastor kissing a young man. Why did no one stand up and speak out? They were afraid of losing their jobs or ruining the reputation of their popular church. The culture of cool overtook the church's commitment to God's calling on their lives.

Swimming against the current of the culture is incredibly difficult work. It is not an easy pursuit and it requires total dedication. Standing out in a world that begs us, cajoles us, even seduces us to be a part of the popular opinion is challenging. It's extraordinary for someone to buck the trend. We will be seen as imprudent if we go against it. How foolish David must have looked taking a slingshot to the battlefield! How crazy Daniel must have seemed when he refused the king's meat. And yet they made the decisions they did for a reason. They weren't simply rejecting trends for the sake of being difficult or different; they were saying no to something that was getting in the way of their pursuit of God's calling.

When you and I decide to stand out not for our own popularity but for the good of others, we move the kingdom closer to earth. Standing out from the crowd does not mean being loud or obnoxious. And it doesn't have to mean that your actions will draw a lot of attention to yourself. But it does mean your desire for justice or to see God move in the earth outweighs your desire to fit comfortably in the mold of the world. Some very popular, very cool things are actually working at odds with the needs of society and could hurt others if we don't draw attention to them and offer a better way. People who are willing to stand out draw our attention to things we miss or ignore. They are willing to take the heat for a new idea or the pressure of standing alongside what's right, even when it goes against popular opinion. Don't be afraid to be someone who is conspicuous because you will not conform to the misguided actions, opinions and desires of the majority.

One area of society where the normal way of life is far from God's heart is the division in our world according to race and culture. I clearly acknowledge the fact that some things are much better today than they were in the past, but the truth remains that we still have a long way to go. In our society, large percentages of people of color live below the poverty line, fill our prisons or have appalling educational choices. America's first black president took office at the same time that the U.S. Senate was left without even one African American senator. There is still work to do.

I do not think that the majority of people are racists or hate one another. Of course there are still very ignorant people, but they do not comprise the majority. I think the majority of people are simply blending into the community around them, which is typically monocultural. People are not typically stretched beyond their everyday experience.

When society is as divided as it is today, crosscultural interactions often cannot happen by accident. We must be intentional about spending time with people of different races and ethnicities. Century-old racial issues will not be solved in a church service or at a conference. Trust is built at ballgames, at birthday parties, on vacations and at happy hour. When we don't spend enough time with people of other races outside of prescribed times, such as work or a special service at church, we don't really know each other. We don't learn to appreciate one another. We aren't able to break down stereotypes or heal from past experiences.

Jim Crow laws, which were enacted at the state and local levels throughout the United States between 1876 and 1965, mandated racial segregation in all public facilities. Supposedly "separate but equal" facilities were provided for black Americans to keep blacks and whites separate from each other. In reality, the resources and accommodations for black citizens were usually vastly inferior to those provided for white citizens, which resulted in systemic economic, educational and social disadvantages for African Americans. Some examples of Jim Crow laws are the segregation of public schools, public places and public transportation, and the segregation of restrooms, restaurants and drinking fountains for whites and blacks. Even the U.S. military was segregated.

State-sponsored school segregation in the United States was declared unconstitutional by the Supreme Court in 1954 in *Brown v. Board of Education*. Generally, the remaining Jim Crow laws were overruled by the Civil Rights Act of 1964 and the Voting Rights Act of 1965. But the damage had already been done. Jim Crow and other laws taught us how to live separately and how to hate one another. When those laws were repealed, we didn't automatically know how to relate or trust. We didn't suddenly start over with everyone given a clean slate. We began in a place of deep-seated hurt, confusion and bitterness.

The church had the opportunity to lead through these delicate issues. In reality, given the teachings on race in the Bible, the church ought to be different, and yet the church is still very segregated. It's sometimes hard to believe that we have so many problems around race in the church, and while I think there have been many attempts to bridge the separation within church walls, the changes have been notoriously slow in coming. Why is the church not farther ahead? An article by Christine A. Scheller titled "Who Gets the Money?" appeared on urbanfaith.com. She asserts that organizations run by African Americans suffer financially due to the very fact that a minority leader is at the helm. The article notes:

> Fred Smith is founder and president of The Gathering, a group that encourages Christian philanthropy. He agrees that lack of trust and latent racism can be factors [in race-based fundraising disparities], but says, "I suspect the predominant cause is a lack of networks that are peer-based." [Christian philanthropist Mark] Soderquist acknowledges the reality that white-led ministries often have an easier time getting funding than black-led ministries. "It's like urban ministry's dirty little secret in that we are often the ones who speak prophetically to the majority culture church about issues of justice and issues of race, and yet we continue to fit into this system where we seem dependent on the white leadership of

organizations." He says it's a catch-22, because inner-city ministries need resources, but funding more easily flows from white resources to white-led organizations.[12]

This documentation of a reality I have often experienced during my more than twenty years in ministry causes me to tear up when I read it. Yet it also makes me very thankful for the many extraordinary people who are not African American but have supported Mission Year and other projects I have led as an African American. My heart is joyful as I think about the donors of many ethnicities I have sat with around the country who consistently support our work. I am appreciative that they stand out from the worldly trends that fund God's work based on racial divides. They are quietly going against a pattern of injustice by trusting a leader of color.

Their example defines a call for us as we seek to be extraordinary and not blend into the trends of society. What ministries am I supporting and who leads them? Are they all one group of people? Do I know of any ministries led by people of color? If not, why not? Can I invite a leader of color to share at my church about the work they do and the needs they have? How can I choose a different path from the one structured around racism that flows through society? If white Christians more consistently stood out and supported their African American brothers and sisters, it would create a new context for the kingdom and offer a new example to the world. Instead, we are following popular trends and therefore offering the same hurt, misunderstandings and pain.

Standing out is not easy by any stretch of the imagination, especially when you're going against the popular flow of society. Still, our small offerings to stand out can change the world. I am proud to say I know and have been with philanthropists that don't follow the trend of the world, and I choose to spread the hope of change by highlighting the great efforts of those who go against the flow. The need in the church is for more extraordinary thinkers like them— people who have surrendered their ordinary lives to a kingdom imagination—who will be intentional about getting to know people who are not like them, and binding their ministries together.

Whether it's to do with our ethnicity or some other aspect of our selves, our kingdom imagination will call us away from blending in to the dominant cultural ideals. We have not been made to be just like one another, but we were made to enhance one another like salt enhances a meal. God created us all with human commonalities, but with different fingerprints that define our uniqueness. In order to follow Christ regardless of societal influences, we must be comfortable being ourselves. The gifts, talents and abilities God has given each of us are made to be celebrated in community, but they also maintain a uniqueness that cannot be denied. Our individuality, not our ability to blend in, is what we offer to the world, and it is what God created in us to be shared. We have been fearfully and wonderfully made. Go ahead and be you. Stand out! Make a difference.

9

Two Kinds of Dreaming

*All men dream but not equally. Those who dream by night in the
dusty recesses of their minds wake in the day to find that it was vanity;
but the dreamers of the day are dangerous men, for they may act
their dream with open eyes to make it possible.*

T. E. LAWRENCE

When I consider a dream, I see a reality waiting to be realized. The
actualized vision is already present. It's alive! It converses
with you and makes you laugh or smile. It invites your creativity and imagination, and it moves you to initiate its physical manifestation. A dream drops into the heart, and it requests entrance into the world through our labor.

A commitment of spirit, mind and body is required for a
dream to materialize. It is no simple endeavor. That is why I
appreciate deeply the notion put forward by T. E. Lawrence:
dreamers of the day, who take their dreams seriously and act
their dreams into reality, are in the process of seeing their
lives become extraordinary.

This kind of dreaming, of course, is different from the dreams we may have of ourselves becoming mutants and saving the world from nuclear disaster. There is a difference between dreams that occur in our thoughts and don't have much to do with reality, and the ones where we sense God calling us to something bigger by the action we take. Dreams of mutants are usually ignored (hopefully), but the ones where we sense God's call may move us to change our lives in a way that offers hope to the world.

True dreaming can be a consuming, risky, and beautiful endeavor. I connect dreaming to a commitment of spirit because I believe God first drops visions into our spirit. God connects with our spirits through pictures of peace, hope, community and shalom—the wellness of the world. The experience shared with the Creator of life can in itself be so life-giving that we can actually become overwhelmed by the moment. It is my belief that such dreams stem directly from God, and that one of his main purposes of imparting dreams is to inspire the pursuit of good for the world.

Dreams cannot end in our spirit. Such an all-encompassing revelation must also begin to marinate in our minds. It is there that we form ideas as we meditate, begin to envision the dream's formation, and picture the end result. It is in this stage that we get excited and inspired. Vision is formed, creativity engaged, and passion is produced. Because the image exists so clearly in the spirit of the dreamer, the mind phase helps this person to articulate and describe the picture so others can also become excited about the new reality. The connection of a dream to the mind is crucial because it creates space to invite the community to dream as well.

The body phase of a dream is a different kind of work. We begin to talk about the dream, make plans and bring others on board. This season is where the hard work begins. It is the messy reality. I say messy because it's where our human element is most involved, and since we are flawed in our best moments, this process is not always neat. Lawrence's night dreamers, those who simply talk of dreams, cannot survive this phase, and the dream quickly fades away. But true dreamers must take action.

In this initiation and activation, chaos may result. Many dreamers, like myself, are not gifted with organizational skills and therefore exacerbate the messiness. We may dream big dreams, but we also have the ability to cause quite the stir in execution phase. This exemplifies another reason to get the community dreaming because then everyone's unique gifts work together to realize God's vision.

In reality, we all dream. We may imagine getting married, owning a boat, starting a business, going to college, visiting another country or running a marathon. You name it, we dream about it. This visioning is a part of the human experience. We are all dreamers, and some of these dreams are realized while some are not. So how do God-given dreams differ from others? I believe there is a calling infused in such dreams to have a deeper meaning.

Ordinary dreaming focuses on the self, while extraordinary dreaming includes others. It's fine to have dreams for ourselves, but when most of those dreams center around our own leisure, family or wealth, I think we lose sight of why

God puts himself in the human spirit through dreams. Dreams are meant to promote goodness and God's glory. We alter their purpose when we only focus on our own desires and hopes. Dreaming of being a doctor in order to serve the world is very different from dreaming of getting wealthy through a medical career. One will have great impact in the lives of others, and the other will do great things for herself.

◆ ◆ ◆

We get off the trolley in Buenos Aires, Argentina, and arrive in one of the poor *villas,* or shantytowns. Imagine a street with a median five yards wide and completely covered with waist-high heaps of unbagged trash and recyclables. Smoke billows from piles of burning ash. We approach the home of Ernesto and Claudia.

Neighborhood entrepreneurs, Ernesto and Claudia have created and oversee a business that collects recyclable material and sells it to large companies. The work is done on the streets; there is no building to hide the work that goes on here as it happens right in front of their home. Loads of old computers, aluminum, steel and plastic bottles line the streets. We sit with Claudia for a few minutes as she explains their business and shares that all the employees are currently on vacation because they give all the men a week off in the summer.

This neighborhood is packed with moms caring for young kids while men pull carts all over town to collect recyclable materials for a living. Ernesto and Claudia employ twenty men. They also support work that happens for the good of others, contributing to after-school and food programs. I sit in a dusty, grassless yard in front of an unfinished, concrete home, and learn how this family supports twenty families with their business and gives to other communities in need.

Ernesto and Claudia obviously know how to run a strong business and supervise employees. They have a contract with larger recycling companies and pick up computers from businesses around town. So why do they live in a shantytown in such a simple house? Entrepreneurs who are considered sophisticated, successful, or respected and admired tend to operate under the assumption that their receipt of the spoils is a crucial aspect of business leadership. In fact, increased profits are how success is measured, and it is typical for a business leader to reveal his achievements by living at a standard that is significantly more desirable than those who work for him. He may drive a nice car to a front-row parking space at the office. His home may be much larger than those of other workers, his clothes much more expensive. Part of the status of business leader has become connected to living a certain high-class lifestyle, regardless of the standard of living for other staff. Why don't Ernesto and Claudia take their talents to the "marketplace" where they will earn more money? They could even be able to give more away, since they obviously have a heart for supporting others. Why do they live near these people? They don't have to do it this way. It seems unsophisticated.

It seems that being extraordinary doesn't mean that you are served by the people who benefit from your leadership and gifts. Ernesto is a great leader and gifted businessman, and he doesn't think about living better than his employees. He dreams of improving life for everyone where he lives by offering men the opportunity to work. He goes even further by teaching them the business, paying them fairly and offering incentives for those who want to grow. He doesn't talk of a better day away from his community, but he speaks of and works toward a better day right where they are together.

This example of extraordinary living is powerfully challenging. Clearly this Argentine couple has chosen to dream dreams on a grander scale than their own benefit. They are blessing their neighbors over and above themselves. That is kingdom work.

I have witnessed extraordinary dreaming in a context where resources were ever-present and a seductive lifestyle calling. But an extraordinary leader listens to dreams God places on the heart over and above the dreams society pushes. There is a cost, however, and that usually comes in the form of personal sacrifice for the dreamer. The price of dreaming is sometimes steep and may be filled with late nights, changes in relationships, and new ways of living that may or may not be understood by people around them. When you and I follow a call we should be mindful that not everyone has heard the same things and may not be willing to modify their lives.

Danny Wuerfful is a beloved friend who I think has been an inspiration. Danny has been a successful football player winning the national championship and the Heisman trophy in college. He was drafted in the fourth round of the NFL draft by the New Orleans Saints. He played with the Saints, Redskins, and Chicago Bears. In the middle of his football career, his life took a turn when he began spending time as a volunteer in New Orleans. Danny began giving time to Desire Street Ministries and learning about God's heart for the poor and his responsibility to the poor as a follower of Jesus. Danny eventually had to answer some questions. He was living his dreams, but God had other plans for his life. And the call from God would eventually take overtake the desire to play football.

> He dreamed of being a professional football player
>   one day
> And so on the path to play he jumped
> Running, training, weight lifting galore,
> He dreamed of being a professional football player
>   one day
> And on the path he jumped,
> Practice, practice, and practice some more,
> He dreamed of being a professional football player
>   one day
> And so on the path he jumped,
> Hurts, strains and all kind of pains
> He dreamed of being a professional football player
>   one day
> And so on the path he jumped,
> OK games, good games, and great games he played,
> He dreamed of being a professional football player
>   one day,
> And so on the path he jumped,
> More great games, to college he went, and more great
>   games came his way,

He dreamed of being a professional football player
　　one day,
And so on the path he jumped,
Super games came his way, Heisman trophy, national
　　champs, top pick in the draft,
He dreamed of being a professional football player
　　one day
And so on the path he jumped
His dreams came true this day, NFL player and on
　　his way,
He is a professional football player this day,
Until God spoke and led his heart astray,
And on the path he jumped,
Serve those whose dreams are fading away, where
　　poverty and hopelessness rule the day,
He is a professional football player today,
Those whom he could help because his dreams came
　　true, come serve the kingdom was the call,
And on the path he jumped
He is not a professional football player today
But changing the world because he offered his gifts,
Super games everyday, because the author of his
　　dreams is the one he lifts.

This is the story of a dear friend whose dream to play professional football did come true. However, one day God asked
him clearly to commit his life to service instead of going back
to the NFL. He turned his dreams over to God, and God is
using that submission in powerful ways to promote the kingdom glory.

What are your dreams? Who do they benefit most? Are they dreams of wealth and riches for you to relax and enjoy life or are they dreams for you to change the world? There is a way for your dreams for yourself to convert to dreams for the kingdom. Give them back to God. He is the Creator of dreams from the very beginning. Place your dreams on the altar and let God use them to change you and the world.

God promises as much.

"In the Last Days," God says, "I will pour out my Spirit on every kind of people: Your sons will prophesy, also your daughters; Your young men will see visions, your old men dream dreams." (Acts 2:17 *The Message*)

What a beautiful picture of the spirit of God at work through the dreaming of his people!

10

Money

How much of you does God have? Does He have all of you?
Does He have your dreams? Your desires? Your possessions?
God wants to do a work in our hearts.
He wants to make us generous.

ROBERT MORRIS

Thirty percent of Jesus' parables taught about money. Society spends a great deal of its words on money as well. Think of any band or artist you enjoy, no matter the genre—country, hip hop, rock, indie, whatever. I have a strong suspicion you can think of *at least* one of their songs that talks about money, whether having a lot, not having enough, or wanting more. Money talk is all around us, and yet what we choose to do with our money continues to be a very private matter for most people.

Christians, even those who value community or believe that God cares about all details of our lives, seem to maintain an attitude around the checkbook that this is their own personal business. Money continues to be a main factor leading to divorces, yet we still do not invite others to join into our financial lives for teaching, encouragement or challenge. Yes, we may hear messages at church on the sensitive topic, but those tend to stay relegated to the 10 percent that "belongs to God." There seems to be a pass with the other 90 percent of your check which, as long as it's not illegal, you may spend however you want.

Other Christian teachings around money suggest that steering clear of credit card debt is a good idea and encourage saving and investing for the future. Our society prides itself on building up nest eggs. Until recently, few were actually seeking to reduce their debt and increase their savings, but the conversation around these practices has been going on for a while. What is often missing from these money discussions is true training around becoming givers, investing money in kingdom projects and blessing others, particularly the poor.

Society equates money with power. The more green you have, the more influence you are given. In all kinds of businesses, ministries or project committees, whether you're building a church, opening a restaurant or sending relief workers to Haiti, money is often the controlling factor in the room. The one holding the almighty dollar is often afforded the opportunity to have the final say. Wars have been waged, friends have turned their backs on one another, churches have split, children kidnapped, human rights denied and leaders fallen—all for money. Its meaning and purpose in our lives has been misplaced, and as followers of Jesus, we absolutely must be different in the way we manage the money with which God has entrusted us.

How do we, seeking to follow Christ in a world obsessed with money, stand out? Organizations have developed to help people and organizations grow in stewardship. Many are doing fine work, but I think we need to go a bit deeper. So much of our human experience is shaped by money—whether we have it or not, been hurt by someone with it, taken it from someone or had someone take it from us. How do we become extraordinary when it comes to money? I think there are responses to money that exemplify the extraordinary presence of Christ. We can learn from these examples where we see God pleased with the actions of his people.

No doubt if you attended children's programming at your church, then you are familiar with the Good Samaritan. Jesus is asked who we should consider as our neighbors when we seek to love our neighbor as ourselves. He responds with a story. A man is beaten up and lying beside the road in obvious need. A priest and a religious Levite pass him by with barely a thought. Then the man is seen by a Samaritan. This passerby helps him bandage his wounds, takes him to an inn for care and then offers to pay for any future expenses that may occur while the man is being cared for well. Responding to the ruler who first asked the question "Who is my neighbor?" Jesus presents this portrait of a good neighbor and commands him to go and do likewise.

We see extraordinary giving in this story. It manifests with three principles. First, the Samaritan witnesses obvious need, and responds immediately and personally. He has the means to help the beaten man both financially and with actions, and he responds with both.

We also observe the Samaritan put the wounded person before himself as he walks while the injured man rides on his donkey. The person in need of aid is more comfortable during the journey, and the Samaritan is inconvenienced in the process.

Third, the Samaritan makes arrangements for ongoing care, so that the wounded man will have ample time to heal without worry. The innkeeper is directed to provide proper care and to send the bill to the Samaritan. If we responded immediately to instances of need with financial and personal assistance, put others' needs before our own, and made sure we provided ongoing care, we would be more than simply financial donors; we would be true neighbors with those in need. This is extraordinary giving that we behold in the story of the Good Samaritan.

We also witness an encounter with Jesus that affects the checkbook. Zacchaeus was a tax collector who heard Jesus was coming to town and wanted to see for himself what all the fuss about. He had probably heard of the miracles Jesus was performing and seen the crowds that surrounded him. Tax collectors were not favored among the people—they were known for being a bit shady in their dealings by collecting more from the people than they really owed and pocketing the profit after they paid the government their percentage—so it is doubtful that anyone went out of his way to help Zacchaeus see, even though he was small in stature. Therefore, he decided to take matters into his own hands and climb a tree to see Jesus.

This was probably a crazy scene because a wealthy, adult man is seen shimmying up a tree to try and sneak a peek at a famous teacher. When Jesus spots Zacchaeus in the tree, he asks him to come down and then announces he is going to his home for dinner. Everyone, including the disciples, is stunned that Jesus would ask to dine with a sinner. People were used to seeing dishonest Zacchaeus show up at their door to collect money, and now here is Jesus, a moral teacher, showing up at Zacchaeus's house for a meal.

When Jesus acknowledged him and invited himself into his home, it blew Zacchaeus away. It changed his life there on the spot, and he showed his change in dramatic fashion. In that very moment, Zacchaeus announced that he would give half his wealth to the poor and pay back anyone he has cheated four times what he took. Zacchaeus's response represents a complete surrender to Jesus. He was not holding back anything, especially his finances. Money was no longer the controlling factor in this man's life. Perhaps all along Zacchaeus was seeking the acceptance that Jesus offered him that afternoon. Perhaps money was substituting for a deeper need, and when Jesus addressed the true heart of the matter, money became something to be used to help others.

In media today—songs, movies, TV shows—we see many people putting their hope in money. The common thought is that all life needs is more money than what we have. Maybe we have placed too much emphasis on the dollar and not enough on Jesus. Perhaps we are looking for money to meet our deepest human needs, and it never seems like enough. That's because it isn't!

When people find their worth in Jesus, they find their ordinary lives becoming extraordinary. There is no other thing in the world that can bring the kind of hope and acceptance like he can. Money, by contrast, loses its power. It no longer has a mighty grip as the major source that makes things happen. We cease to chase it, put our hopes in it, or sell each other down the river for it. Zacchaeus's response to give half his money to the poor is interesting. Once he was freed from the captivity, he no longer needed to control it and could lavishly give it where it was needed. Extraordinary people are careful to keep money in proper perspective. It simply becomes a resource to help move the kingdom along. It is not needed for identity, direction or power.

Another common biblical passage when discussing money is that of the rich, young ruler. Let's examine the story in Luke 18:18-25:

> One day one of the local officials asked him, "Good Teacher, what must I do to deserve eternal life?"
>
> Jesus said, "Why are you calling me good? No one is good—only God. You know the commandments, don't you? No illicit sex, no killing, no stealing, no lying, honor your father and mother."
>
> He said, "I've kept them all for as long as I can remember."
>
> When Jesus heard that, he said, "Then there's only one thing left to do: Sell everything you own and give it away to the poor. You will have riches in heaven. Then come, follow me."
>
> This was the last thing the official expected to hear.

He was very rich and became terribly sad. He was holding on tight to a lot of things and not about to let them go. Seeing his reaction, Jesus said, "Do you have any idea how difficult it is for people who have it all to enter God's kingdom? I'd say it's easier to thread a camel through a needle's eye than get a rich person into God's kingdom." (*The Message*)

The rich young ruler is a difficult story because we see a harsh reality: money can invade our hearts and keep us from God. Christ had access to all resources and didn't need the young man's money for the poor. He could access any amount of money for his use. The tragedy for this man was that his heart, unlike Zaccheaus's, would not submit to Jesus and experience freedom from the control of money. Dollars and cents, when they take over our lives, will leave us empty and craving more. The rich young ruler had to make a choice, and he chose to keep his cash. Life was too good for him. What would he do if he didn't have his riches? Money can be a god, and many in this world are worshiping it every minute of every day.

The Bible declares the love of money as the root of all evil. It is not about how much money you have, it is about where your heart is concerning money. There are people in the world with great wealth that do not love money, and there are some people in the world who have nothing and love money. Extraordinary people keep their heart soft toward God and their senses aware to stay far away from loving money. God wants unlimited access to our hearts, regardless of the balance in our bank accounts. Jesus describes money as a master in Luke 16 and declares we cannot serve both riches and God. We need to be reminded regularly of the place of money and its good uses as well as its potential danger. That's why it is also an encouragement to hear modern-day testimonies of extraordinary giving of money.

Some Mission Year team members in Houston encountered an extraordinary man named Don who exemplified a life free from the love of money. The team members first met Don on a Sunday afternoon in the park. Along with others from their church, they had spent many Sundays at a local park, sharing home-cooked food with homeless folks. It isn't a feeding program exactly, but more of a family meal with brothers and sisters who don't have homes. They call it Simple Feast. Don was a regular, and he was never without his sketchpad and pencil.

Early in her Mission Year, Sarah noticed that Don appeared to be sketching her and her teammate while they patiently listened to the long, rambling story of another Simple Feast friend. Later, he approached her and gently offered his drawing. It turned out that Don was not only a talented artist, but he was a kind and thoughtful friend as well. Before long, Don was a frequent visitor at the Mission Year team's house, stopping by to play a board game, share a snack or just talk.

Since their church has an art gallery, team members eventually arranged for Don to display some of his drawings at the church. A few pieces of his art were sold, totaling $250 that went directly to Don. So what did he do? Don promptly donated it all back to the church. Really.

"When Don gave that money," Sarah told me, "I was so

humbled that it brought tears to my eyes. I don't think I would have done the same. I probably would have kept some of the money for myself, justifying it by the fact that art supplies cost money. But Don, who has so little, gave everything. It was so beautiful."

On a trip to Houston, I got to experience Don's generosity—and what Sarah calls his incredible joy—for myself. He complimented me on our Mission Year team's approach to outreach. "These young people really are my friends, and I thank you for sending them here. Keep up the good work!" Wow. I love it that our young people were able to draw this gentle man back into the fellowship of the church and remind him that he has something to give the world. And I love it that he showed them the truth that Jesus keeps trying to show us:

> Just then he looked up and saw the rich people dropping offerings in the collection plate. Then he saw a poor widow put in two pennies. He said, "The plain truth is that this widow has given by far the largest offering today. All these others made offerings that they'll never miss; she gave extravagantly what she couldn't afford—she gave her all!" (Luke 21:1-4 *The Message*)

Don's story encourages me, but he is not alone in his extravagant, extraordinary giving. I met Eric shortly after my wife and I started our first missions organization in Philly. I was volunteering at the Billy Graham crusade that was in town. I am an extrovert and have no problems meeting or talking to anyone new. I started a conversation with Eric, who was also volunteering. Eric was an accountant and owned a firm in Bryn Mawr, a Philadelphia suburb. We hit it off right away and spent a few hours together each evening. The last night of the crusade, we exchanged information and promised to stay in touch.

About a month later we did connect over lunch to catch up. It was at that lunch that Eric told me he would like to support the work our organization was doing with the homeless. I really didn't know how to answer him except to say thank you and that I would get back to him with some ideas. We had never had a donor outside of family and friends who wanted to support this work, so it was very exciting.

Eric became a good friend and a faithful donor. In fact, he got his entire company involved in supporting our work in shelters, as well as another friend and *his* company. Eric was a great teacher for my wife and me as he and his wife exemplified to us the extraordinary purposes of wealth through the ways they gave, not only to the work with the homeless, but also to support our family. They are extraordinary. I was a young man who barely knew anything about running a nonprofit, and a wealthy follower of Jesus offered his life, work and wealth to the Lord. He followed the examples in the Word and, like Zacchaeus, he knew that more important than having money was having a heart to please Jesus.

Where is your heart concerning money? How central is it to your life and work? Do you get your acceptance based on your net worth? What if you had nothing starting today? If you have nothing, do you feel less than others because of your financial situation? Are you extravagantly generous? Does God have your heart?

11

Time

Time is free, but it's priceless. You can't own it,
but you can use it. You can't keep it, but you can spend it.
Once you've lost it you can never get it back.

HARVEY MACKAY

Do you ever feel like people around you are too busy to get to know you?

Do you ever feel like you're too busy to really spend time doing the things you say you want to do?

Our society is plagued by busyness. It is assumed that everyone is excessively busy, and it is taken for granted that this is socially acceptable. If you ask someone for some time these days, it is nearly like asking for gold. We are all familiar with the expression "Time is money." And even for those who aren't utilizing their time simply for creation of profit, there is a reality that time is precious and many of us don't have very much of it to spare.

This all-consuming societal busyness forces us to ask what exactly are we doing. How are we spending our time? As culture has progressed, more and more devices and technological advances have been created to save us time. The microwave and fast food joints were supposed to speed up our meals. Cars (outside of traffic) were supposed to make it quicker to get around town. Watches, day planners and then mobile devices helped us manage time. Text messages are quicker than phone calls. Data plans allow us to check our email while riding the elevator, walking, talking, you name it. We have taken multitasking to entirely new levels. And yet, even with all the time-reducing devices and multiple activities occurring at once, we still collectively complain about lack of time.

In Ephesians 5, the Bible instructs us to redeem time. We are admonished to make good use of it because the times are evil, and it is important that we have a handle on things. The New Living Translation writes it this way:

> So be careful how you live. Don't live like fools, but like those who are wise. Make the most of every opportunity in these evil days. Don't act thoughtlessly, but understand what the Lord wants you to do. (Ephesians 5:15-17)

The unfortunate reality is that many of us are spending our time "thoughtlessly" and simply falling into what the culture makes readily available to us as opportunities to waste our time.

Many of you have probably had the experience where you sit down to study or work . . . and then you check your email . . . and then your Facebook news feed . . . and then you decide to tweet that you are trying to work or study . . . and then you see that a friend has tweeted a blog that looks interesting . . . and then you read it . . . and so it goes. Before you know it, an hour (dare I say more) has passed, and you cannot really account for what you have been doing. Our generation is spending an inordinate amount of time being distracted from the things that matter.

These distractions during work or school pale in comparison to the time we lose at home during our "free" time. The numbers reveal that we are spending more time outside of work watching TV, surfing the internet and playing video games than we do anything else. We are entertaining ourselves to death. There is certainly a healthy space for entertainment in our lives, but there is an unavoidable reality that much of is it just a plain waste of our precious resource of time.

Below are some startling statistics of the hours we are spending each year on entertainment activities.[13]

- 1,555 hours watching television, up from 1,467 in 2000. The estimate includes 678 hours watching broadcast TV and 877 watching cable and satellite.
- 974 hours listening to the radio, up from 942 in 2000.
- 195 hours using the Internet, up from 104.
- 175 hours reading daily newspapers, down from 201.
- 122 hours reading magazines, down from 135.
- 106 hours reading books, down an hour.
- 86 hours playing video games, up from 64.

Let's run our media consumption through Paul's appeal to the Roman church in Romans 12:1 "So here's what I want you to do, God helping you: Take your everyday, ordinary life—your TV-watching, internet surfing, videogame playing life—and place it before God as an offering" (*The Message*). Even the most modern of translations don't include these in the life we can offer God. Why? Because they are simply distractions that waste our time.

The heartbreaking truth is that many of us have already offered our sleeping, eating, going-to-work life to the gods of TV, movies, music and more. It's not uncommon for people to sacrifice sleep, meals or even work so that they can watch one more show or play one more game. God has so much more for us.

Some individuals are not wasting their time, so much as filling it . . . constantly. These people may have no time for entertainment pursuits and are hopelessly behind in *The Office* or *Jersey Shore* references because they are so incredibly busy. Perhaps they have a workaholic-like commitment to their jobs. They log sixty-hour work weeks religiously, and they never feel completely "off the clock." Blackberries and iPhones have simply allowed these people to keep working at all hours of the day and night, regardless of office location. Someone who strives to fill all their time may have a handle on their job, but may over-commit to church or ministry opportunities, volunteer efforts or clubs, classes and projects.

This type of busyness is different from days filled with entertainment, but it still forces questions to be asked. Do we really *need* to be so busy, or do we *like* it? Why? Does a jam-packed calendar make us feel needed, loved, approved? Do we not trust others to do tasks and need to keep ourselves involved in every project? Do we really think things cannot get done without our input? Or does the list of obligations make us feel fulfilled? When someone asks for our time and we have to say no, do we feel superior? Is it more important to us to be busy than to actually be productive or complete work? Are we afraid of solitude . . . of being still . . . of quiet? Are we afraid that in the silence our voices of insecurity, doubt and discouragement will have space to speak? Are we scared that if the meetings stop we'll find ourselves alone? What is pushing us to add more and more to our schedules?

We must ask the questions. God has plans for our time, and we don't want to miss it being busy with unimportant, or even very important, tasks that distract us from our extraordinary purpose. What creative expressions or world-shaking solutions is society missing because the people called to contribute those to us are too distracted, too obligated or too loud to move forward?

God wants to redeem our time. He wants to saturate our days with activities that truly matter. When we distract ourselves with entertainment or with obligations the world values, we may be bypassing opportunities for creating, learning or deepening relationships. While we may be tempted to do otherwise and we witness others doing differently, these endeavors have kingdom value and offer an investment return for the time that we commit.

I believe one of the reasons we are so drawn to music, movies, and television is because we have a natural longing for creative expression. The storytelling, the characters and the emotional journeys—however juvenile or sophisticated—draw us in and connect with our creative selves. The time these mediums rob from us, however, often prevent us from engaging the creative energies Christ has placed within us. Imagine if David had been too caught up in action movies to pen the Psalms. Or what if Mary had spent her pregnancy consuming soap operas and never writing her praise song? Working with our hands, telling stories, capturing human emotion, these are important creative endeavors that can bless the heart of God and point others toward Christ. But many such creative works are left unfinished in society today while the artists are updating their Facebook profiles.

Learning is another way we are offered opportunities to redeem our time on earth. This practice can take two forms. The first is the more traditional track of learning new information or skills, which often connect back to our creativity, such as learning to play the guitar, taking a photography class or joining a writing group. Other times, we seek to learn more about society through studying politics and cultures or about God's world by exploring new knowledge of animals or trees. But our learning can also contribute to our relationships, such as studying a new language to connect with immigrants to our city, taking a cooking class to increase our confidence in hospitality, or acquiring a skill like quilting that has brought communities of women together for decades. Committing to learning engages our mind and spirit as we grow and develop in ways that please God.

Another practice of learning is the sacred time spent seeking to know more of God. Hours spent in prayer, studying the Word, serving others in God's name or worshiping the king is time spent in kingdom activities. The Bible is a living text that can never be fully known, meaning that we can never exhaust the benefits we gain from reading its pages. God wants to speak to us, but we are filling our time with noise and activity to the point that we can never hear him. "Be still, and know that I am God," he tells us in Psalm 46:10. This is an invitation we should not ignore.

In our busyness and distractions, we are missing the sacred relationships that are all around us. In a world where everyone boasts hundreds of friends in online communities, loneliness is ever-present. Depression and self-focus are all too common. As extraordinary people, we are called out of that norm. We have the opportunity to create true community that makes time for others. We can be individuals who prioritize others and can stop what we're doing to listen to a friend in need, celebrate when others are rejoicing, and comfort when someone is mourning. Extraordinary people have a God-given openness that allows them to avoid suspiciousness, competitiveness or pride in relationships, but seeks to welcome others into God-saturated relationship. Time spent on porches, in kitchens and walking together is time invested in the kingdom.

We have been called to combat evil. If we recognize the amount of grace in our lives and how that grace keeps us from destroying ourselves, then we are compelled to spread that good news. The grace we have been afforded through Jesus has set us free, and we are now on the other side of evil. Sharing the good news of that grace is time invested in the kingdom.

Wasting our time is a weapon of the enemy. When we simply tell ourselves "one more show," "one last movie," "one final game," it is a victory for evil because these are all ploys to keep us from redeeming the time. When we spend our time well, it is an assault on the kingdom of evil. One more prayer, one more hour of study, one more conversation with a friend—these are all weapons in our hands to advance the kingdom of God.

I have been blessed to bear witness to an extraordinary couple who knew how to offer their time as an offering to God. The Andersons were leaders at our church, as well as with various organizations around the city. They taught Bible study, led youth group, were deacons at the church, and advised men's and women's groups. They both also worked full-time jobs. If you start adding up the time, you begin to ask how it was possible that two people could get so much done and at such levels of quality. They were definitely busy, but their lives were dedicated to serving Jesus well, and it showed in everything they did.

Since the Andersons served as youth directors when I was a teen, I got an up-close view of how they stewarded their time. I spent countless hours in their home as they hosted youth meetings, dinners, rap sessions and holiday celebrations. I always found it odd that the Andersons had this wonderful home, but in their living room there was no TV. There was a small one in their basement that barely worked. Believe me, we tried to rig it up many times for youth group events, but to no avail.

The Andersons spent very little time being entertained.

They had set their home up in a way that revealed their primary priority of connecting with others. Without a TV in the main room, many great conversations occurred that were never distracted by commercials or juvenile dialogue. They also highly valued learning. The same basement with the tiny TV held walls and walls of books, and often when I visited Deacon Anderson, he was downstairs reading. But he did not stop with his own knowledge. Deacon Anderson constantly stressed the importance of learning all you could. He would challenge us to read and study Scripture, as well as other books, to broaden our view on the world. His library was open to all, and I often met others at his home that were studying or asking him questions. The Andersons were some of the wisest people I knew, and their knowledge of the Bible would blow me away. This couple helped shape a large part of who I am as a follower of Jesus.

Extraordinary people understand time and how to use it wisely. Entertainment has its place, but certainly not a central one in our lives. People are God's greatest creation, and taking time to listen to each other's stories, share in pain, join in celebration and challenge weaknesses is incredibly fulfilling. Taking time to grow as teachers and mentors makes an extraordinary impact in the life of others. Investing our time in God-glorifying creativity, constant learning and deepening relationships contributes to the kingdom experience on earth. That's what the Andersons exemplified for me: incredible teachers who were disciplined enough to limit their entertainment and needless obligation to create time for learning, teaching and spending real time getting to know me and love me during a crucial season in my life.

Where are you spending your God-given time? Are you wasting your life being entertained on your couch? Are you insatiably filling a calendar to feel important? Do you have space to pursue creative thoughts and projects? Are you learning about things that interest you? Are you actively seeking knowledge of God? How are your relationships? Are you spending the time needed to truly care for others? Are you teaching or mentoring? What time are you wasting that you can redirect toward activities that grow the kingdom?

12

The Response

Therefore, I urge you, brothers and sisters, in view of God's mercy, to offer your bodies as a living sacrifice, holy and pleasing to God—this is your true and proper worship. Do not conform to the pattern of this world, but be transformed by the renewing of your mind. Then you will be able to test and approve what God's will is—his good, pleasing and perfect will.

ROMANS 12:1-2

We have come full circle, arriving back at the Scripture that led us to ask the questions about what it means to surrender our ordinary lives. And the final half of this verse suggests that if we offer ourselves, then we will be able to test and prove that God is really good. This is quite the implication! What is being put forth here is the assertion that if we trust God with our lives and turn our backs on this world, then he will prove who he is. If we are the ones needing God's help, then God invites us to try him. If God truly is all who we say we believe that he is, then we have no reason to conform to this world. We are far better off going along with his extraordinary plan, offering up ourselves and our everyday lives, and watching him go to work.

You may feel there is a lot risk in turning your life over to God. We are not just talking about a prayer here or some time on Sunday or even 10 percent of our incomes. We are getting to the nitty gritty, talking about submitting the little, everyday things that we currently try to control, make our own decisions about or simply keep to ourselves. He is asking for those parts of our lives. If we willingly choose to let go of our eating, sleeping and going-to-work pieces of our lives, *those* are the areas God will use to change us. God will transform those ordinary, mundane life moments and use them to impact the world. Our God is extraordinary, and he will use our lives for his incredible purposes.

For some of us, our life as we know it is going pretty well. We followed directions and did things the right way. We saved money, didn't take unnecessary risk, bought our home and have little to no debt. We landed a decent job with good benefits, got married, are raising sweet kids and go to church each week. From the outside, we have the perfect, expected life. Many times, the simple reality is that it doesn't really require God to create a happy, ordinary American life. But God wants to do so much more in your life. He doesn't just want to get along in the world. God wants to reign in the world, overtaking darkness and establishing his kingdom. He has come to bring life and life that is truly abundant. Extraordinary.

There is an invitation here to follow the lead of a little boy on a mountainside. He thought ahead. He followed his mother's directions and packed a lunch. He anticipated his needs and he met them for himself. He was taken care of. Then Jesus asked the little boy to trust him and surrender his everyday, ordinary lunch—his fish and loaves. God performed a miracle that allowed such an ordinary gift to bless the multitude. Through the lunch the boy planned for himself, God used it so that everyone could eat, including the little boy. God is now asking for your lunch. He's asking that you trust him to feed the crowds with your offering and to meet your needs as well.

Others of us cannot relate to the idea of having life in order. Our lives don't make sense and just feel to be one never-ending struggle after another never-ending struggle. Even in our sleep, our brains are working to try and make ends meet. At every chance, we try another strategy to dig out the hole where we find ourselves, but our efforts are fruitless. We just never seem to be on top of our difficulties. Debt piles up, bill collectors keep calling, and the job just doesn't pay enough to cover it all.

These struggles, even in their seriousness, are also ordinary. The God of heaven wants you to live an extraordinary life. He's inviting you to relinquish the worry and the stress into his hands. He's asking you to trust him with your needs. He is reaching out his hand to take hold of your problems, and he promises to transform your life and use your ordinary gifts in his grand purposes.

Regardless of your life situation, you may be convinced that God cannot use your life. *That's great,* you think to yourself, *for those other people.* But maybe you are convinced that while your life is not extraordinary, it is certainly not ordinary. Ordinary is equated with normal, and you have a list of reasons your life cannot be transformed by God. You feel disqualified from this invitation. Perhaps others have told you that you are worthless to the world, to them and even to God. Maybe your mother abandoned you, etching in your heart a sense of being undesirable. Maybe you were arrested. Maybe you needed money, so you slept with one man, but then it never stopped. Maybe you made bad grades and have been told you are stupid. Maybe your dad came in your room at night and violated you. Maybe you tried crack once and found yourself hooked. Maybe someone beats you. Maybe you're too old or too young. Maybe you slept with someone once and contracted HIV. Maybe you thought it was an innocent date and someone forced himself on you. Maybe a coworker betrayed you and left you bitter as you packed up your office. Maybe you grew up in the city or the country. Maybe you got kicked out of school. Maybe someone stole your virginity. Maybe you made a mistake with your money. Maybe you slept with someone one time and became a mother. Maybe a trusted friend deserted you. Maybe a teacher told you that you'd never amount to anything. Maybe your credit score is too low. Maybe it's your gender, or the color of your skin. Maybe it's your experiences, or the experience you haven't had.

Whatever your reason for deciding that you are disqualified from an extraordinary life with Christ, know that God does not disqualify people. He only qualifies. God did not enter into the world to condemn; rather, he came to freely offer grace. Our response to his invitation is the only thing we can do, and our response and participate in his plans can absolutely change the world.

Society loves to focus on the "best of the best" and promote the idea that it is the elite that make a difference in this world. I would like to offer a different view. Jesus did not come for society's celebrities or heroes, because these hierarchies do not exist in God's eyes. We are all broken sinners in need of his grace. We are told explicitly in 1 Corinthians 1:26-31:

> Take a good look, friends, at who you were when you got called into this life. I don't see many of "the brightest and the best" among you, not many influential, not many from high-society families. Isn't it obvious that God deliberately chose men and women that the culture overlooks and exploits and abuses, chose these "nobodies" to expose the hollow pretensions of the "somebodies"? That makes it quite clear that none of you can get by with blowing your own horn before God. Everything that we have—right thinking and right living, a clean slate and a fresh start—comes from God by way of Jesus Christ. That's why we have the saying, "If you're going to blow a horn, blow a trumpet for God." (*The Message*)

God uses whoever is willing to offer themselves to him. There is no such thing as a top candidate. Those who have qualified themselves need not apply. God accepts us in our brokenness, which allows us to give God all the glory because we are so aware that we could not have been involved in such extraordinary experiences in our own strength.

It's possible we don't expect God to do much with our lives because we have subscribed to a silent belief of what I like to call "trickle-down Jesus." You may have heard the phrase "trickle-down economics," a slogan that originated during the Great Depression and was popularized by Ronald Reagan during his time as U.S. president. The basic premise was a position of creating policy and tax benefits for businesses with the expectation that these changes would "trickle down" and positively benefit the general populace. Jobs would be created, and society would care for the poor. It's a controversial stance, but I don't bring it up for a political debate. I bring it up because I believe many of us have implemented this same philosophy when we consider how the world will become a better place and how Christ's message is delivered. We often assume that only those at the top of religious life, such as clergy, are offered the message of the cross, and then we expect that it will "trickle down" to the rest of us.

Please do not misunderstand. I am a pastor with a seminary education, and I wholeheartedly believe that there is a gift of pastoring vital to the church. But do we ever look for ways God might choose to move outside of the seminary campus or pastor's office? I wonder if we have hindered the spread of the gospel by limiting the responsibility to those in religious positions. Exalting clergy in such a way has a danger of corrupting this gift as well. I believe God wants to use each and every ordinary life to accomplish his purposes.

This call is not relegated to those who have committed to full-time ministry. Once again, he does not consider our qualifications, but his plans. By working through "nobodies," it is assured that all trumpets will be blown for God!

I found myself empty one ordinary Wednesday evening. I had become a young man who was not trustworthy because my only goal was having fun. I was not dedicated to anything or anyone because the only person who was important to me was me. My anger prevented me from being teachable, and I used my brain to be slick and quick, not to learn. I had hurt so many young ladies around me, that I was no longer even liked. I was a complete and utter mess.

Even in the house of God, I relied on my experience of putting on a good face in front of church folks. Underneath the smile, however, there was anger, blame, resentment, confusion, sin and probably much more bottled up inside me. I did not like myself very much. But rather than study myself, it was easier to blame and resent others for everything that was going on in and around me. My exterior remained the façade of the good church boy, but I was lying to myself and everyone around me. Looking back, I imagine the adults around me knew my duplicity, but they trusted I would change. They saw something in me that I could not.

It's likely that my mom asked me to go to Bible study that Wednesday, because I don't know how I ended up there. However I got there, I paid no attention to the lesson. Still, God was there and I knew he was calling. I was feeling horrible about life, and everything felt messed up. Meanwhile, God was asking me to offer my life to him. This very life I had made a mess of, the life I thought I could handle on my own, the life that had so much potential that I was wasting away—God was asking me for it. I didn't know why he would want me, and I could not understand why he would not just leave me alone. Honestly, I thought I would appreciate being left alone so that I wouldn't feel guilt when I did something wrong.

God's Spirit was alive and present that night, and he was relentlessly tugging at me. I could hear him asking me to turn over my life. He was assuring me that he could do more with it than I had been doing. I began crying uncontrollably, surrendering in my heart. That Wednesday evening in the basement of the Mt. Zion Baptist church, I gave in to God. I had said the "big prayer" years before as a child, but this surrender was different. I was committing my totally unqualified self to God, submitting to whatever he wanted to do with my ordinary offerings. I felt so broken and desired peace above all else, so I promised my life in exchange for his peace. And I got the better end of the deal.

Why don't you drop your life on God? It is not all smooth-sailing when you offer yourself, but you are held in the hands of one who is greater than you. A peace beyond all understanding is available to you. I can testify that it truly has kept my heart and mind. God wants to do a powerful work in your life. He also wants to include you and your everyday life in world-shaking adventures.

Our world is absolutely in need of the presence of a loving God. If we offer ourselves to him as the body of Christ, turn our backs on the crazy systems of this world, and trust God to meet our needs, the world won't be the same. God will go forth and accomplish his extraordinary purposes through ordinary people like you and me. There can be water and food for everyone who needs it if Christians offer their full selves. I believe homelessness and war can be eliminated. I imagine a world free of nuclear weapons and suicide killings. I believe God has plans to eradicate drugs and to revitalize children's education. I believe God can end racism and terrorism. But I do not believe any of this will happen unless we submit our ordinary, everyday lives to God for him to accomplish his purposes in and through us.

Will you surrender yours?

Notes

[1]Shirin Taber, "Trapped by the Search for Significance," February 24, 2010, <www.relevantmagazine.com/god/deeper-walk/features/20665 -trapped-by-the-search-for-significance>.

[2]"U.S. Job Satisfaction Hits 22-Year Low," <http://money.cnn.com/2010 /01/05/news/economy/job_satisfaction_report/>.

[3]Rosa Parks, in *Sisters in the Struggle,* ed. Bettye Collier-Thomas and Vincent C. Franklin (New York: New York University Press, 2001), p. 61.

[4]Sean Gladding, "Story," session one in *The Story of God, the Story of Us: Video Series* (Downers Grove, Ill.: InterVarsity Press, 2011).

[5]The Barna Group, "Most Twentysomethings Put Christianity on the Shelf Following Spiritually Active Teen Years," <www.barna.org/barna -update/article/16-teensnext-gen/147-most-twentysomethings-put -christianity-on-the-shelf-following-spiritually-active-teen-years>.

[6]"Spirituality in Higher Education," UCLA Higher Education Research Institute, cited at <www.conversantlife.com/theology/how-many-youth -are-leaving-the-church?print=true>.

[7]Joelyn Newcomb, "Bush at Yale: A 'C' Student's Path," letter to the editor, *New York Times,* May 22, 2001, <www.nytimes.com/2001/05/23/ opinion/l-bush-at-yale-a-c-student-s-path-452769.html>.

[8]"Ten Ways to Instantly Build Self-Confidence," <www.pickthebrain .com/blog/10-ways-to-instantly-build-self-confidence/>.

[9]Donald Miller, "How to Get Confidence from God," <http://donmilleris .com/2010/04/28/the-real-way-god-gives-you-confidence/>.

[10]Dietrich Bonhoeffer, *The Cost of Community* (New York: Touchstone, 1995), p. 58.

[11]For a compelling challenge to how relationships in contemporary culture too often take a back seat to other values, read Christopher Heuertz and Christine Pohl, *Friendship at the Margins* (Downers Grove, Ill.: InterVarsity Press, 2010).

[12]Christine A. Scheller, "Who Gets the Money?" <www.urbanfaith.com /2011/02/who-gets-the-money.html/>.

[13]"After Breathing, Americans Spend Most of Their Time Consuming Media," <www.foxnews.com/story/0,2933,236706,00.html>.

ABOUT THE AUTHOR

Leroy Barber is president of Mission Year and CEO of FCS Urban Ministries in Atlanta. He pastors Community Life Church and serves on the boards of Word Made Flesh and the Christian Community Development Association (CCDA). Leroy is the author of *New Neighbor: An Invitation to Join Beloved Community* and a contributor to the groundbreaking book *unChristian: What a New Generation Thinks About Christianity and Why It Matters.*

Leroy is married to Donna; together they have five children.

ABOUT MISSION YEAR

Mission Year is a national urban initiative introducing eighteen- to twenty-nine-year-olds to missional and communal living in the under-resourced city centers of the United States. Mission Year team members spend a year in a neighborhood, building relationships with their neighbors in order to move them closer to whom and where God wants them to be. In the beginning that may mean walking around the block, introducing themselves to people, and later stopping back to ask for prayer requests, share opportunities or just hang out with new friends. Meaningful relationships develop over time, so that eventually team members find themselves deeply involved with their neighbors' lives, helping to meet all kinds of practical needs, and sharing their faith in a very natural way.

To apply to join a Mission Year team, or to contribute to Mission Year financially, visit www.missionyear.org.

LIKEWISE. *Go and do.*

A man comes across an ancient enemy, beaten and left for dead. He lifts the wounded man onto the back of a donkey and takes him to an inn to tend to the man's recovery. Jesus tells this story and instructs those who are listening to "go and do likewise."

Likewise books explore a compassionate, active faith lived out in real time. When we're skeptical about the status quo, Likewise books challenge us to create culture responsibly. When we're confused about who we are and what we're supposed to be doing, Likewise books help us listen for God's voice. When we're discouraged by the troubled world we've inherited, Likewise books encourage us to hold onto hope.

In this life we will face challenges that demand our response. Likewise books face those challenges with us so we can act on faith.

likewisebooks.com